Understanding Soul Winning

By: Tim Downs

Understanding Soul Winning
Copyright © 2011
By: Tim Downs

All scripture references are taken from the *King James Version* of the Bible.

Special thanks to Amanda Bishop Foster for an incredible job editing this book.

Cover design by Denise Cole of Denise Cole Graphics
www.denisecolegraphics.com

For author contact & order information:
Evangelist Tim Downs
Gowinsouls.com
tim@gowinsouls.com

Printed in the USA
By Instantpublisher.com

Dedication

This book is dedicated to my loving wife and my awesome family, all of which have joined together in our burden to win the lost across this World. I am thankful for the sacrifices that they have made to see others saved without ever complaining or allowing any selfishness to stop the cause of reaching out.

My Pastor, Bishop Jack Cunningham, who has allowed his vision, passion, and anointing to seep down to this undeserving vessel.

Bishop & Sister Kenneth Haney who have led by example in reaching the lost and casting vision, along with letting the fire and anointing of the Holy Ghost lead the Apostolic movement into the end-time era!

Evangelist Matt Maddix for having the vision to reach this world and for preaching "Addicted To Soul Winning."

G.A. and Vesta Mangun, Anthony and Mickey Mangun from Alexandria, Louisiana, for leading the way in passion and reaching the lost! You all have inspired me in many ways!

Pastor and Sister Gene Eastlering from Ashland, Kentucky, for giving amazing friendship, believing in our ministry, and providing us a place to stay while God spoke the words of this book into my heart!

Forewords

I've often closed my eyes and deeply meditated on the words, "Go ye into all the world and preach the gospel to every creature," as an attempt to feel the passion that Jesus must have spoken with. I'm a man that's been marked by the burden and heartbeat of Jesus Christ. Only those that have lain on their faces, weeping with broken hearts for the millions without God can understand fully what's been written about in this book. We need the body of Christ to awaken with a fresh passion to simply go win souls.

We are racing towards the rapture of the church, and Jesus is soon to come. We must work while it is day, give while we have time, and take massive action in reaching lost humanity. We don't have time to argue about what method is right or debate about style or approach. We must simply humble ourselves and realize that it always has been and always will be about, "The Father's Business." His business, priority, and passion is soul winning.

I'm so thankful that we have a book, written by a man of experience as well as passion, about soul winning. I am thankful we can get this into the hands of every apostolic believer. Ladies and gentlemen, this is our finest hour and the harvest is plenteous. We have the ability to reach the world if we are willing to Go. We are no longer waiting on God, rather God is waiting on us, to go into the prisons, homeless shelters, juvenile detention centers, courthouses, college campuses, ghettos, highways, byways, hedges, and into the entire world to bring this precious gospel to every creature.

I'm thankful for the ministry and passion of Tim Downs. I've known Tim for over six years, and I've never met a man more committed by his actions to the cause of soul winning. Some say that to become a master, one must put in a minimum of 10,000 hours of practice. I know beyond a shadow of a doubt that the man burning a consuming passion to reach the lost that has written this book has spent well over 10,000 hours in the trenches of evangelism, pulling souls out of hell. Please read this book and allow God to speak to you and give you the same heart for souls.

Tim Downs has traveled hundreds of thousands of miles across the world to inspire and train soul winners. He has given, sacrificed, labored, and proven that these methods work. God has given him great favor and revival. He has been a very effective soul winner and true New Testament evangelist. I wish we had about 1 million other believers that had the same drive and passion. I'm convinced there wouldn't be a lost person on earth if we could get every Holy Ghost-filled believer to have at least half of Tim's passion for souls. I highly recommend this book to anyone that desires to win and disciple souls.

- Matt Maddix, Soul Winners Boot Camp

As a pastor and even a saint of God, I believe that all people realize the importance of reaching the lost. The frustrating part is not understanding *how* to win souls. My biggest frustrations as a pastor were when I would hear messages about the great *End Time Revival* that God was going to pour out. Everyone would get excited and fired up. But then when they returned to their city where God had called them, the end result was always the same, more frustrations and a sense of failure. The reason for this failure is simple. We would hear how God wants to give revival but never told *how* to get it. It's easy to get excited about soul winning but you have to equip people with simple, effective tools to reach to the lost.

I feel Brother Downs' book, *Understanding Souls Winning*, is a must-read book for every Apostolic. In this book, you will find

5

proven, effective tools to help you do what God has called each and every one of us to do, and that is to win souls. The methods in this book have been used across America and across the world. They work in small towns and large towns. You will find everything in this book that you need to be an effective soul winner.

Three years ago, I had the privilege to meet the Downs family. I believe that the Lord spoke to me to bring them to Ashland, Kentucky, where I pastor, to teach us how to have revival. I was very hungry and desperately desired to see God save the city in which he had called me. When the Downs family came to Ashland in November, 2007, we were running 31 people, including the children. Brother Downs began to give our church an understanding of soul winning. He taught us the "Heaven or Hell" method, effective programs to reach more people, and how to disciple the precious souls that we won. The results have been simply amazing.

In the last three years we have baptized over 800 people and over 700 have received the baptism of the Holy Ghost! Our church has grown to an average attendance of around 200 people. We have started a daughter work averaging 50-60. God has done tremendous things in the city of Ashland, Kentucky. We go out on outreach every Thursday and every Saturday, passing out "Blessing Our Community" invitations and also doing the "Heaven or Hell" method. There is no one that I know who is more passionate about reaching the lost than Tim Downs and his family. God has given him simple, effective tools that have sparked revival in countless churches across this world. As you read this book, please ask God to speak to your heart and give you and understanding of how to reach the lost.

- Gene Easterling, pastor of Christian Faith Outreach in Ashland, Kentucky

Preface

I write this book today in hopes of instructing, encouraging, and impacting others to do their very best to reach this lost world.

I was not raised in a church family. Many times my life was hopelessly headed to destruction. It was only through the grace of God that I am here to share some of my burden and passion to see others saved.

I have failed God many times; I am not by any means a perfect man nor have I lived a sinless life. I have, however, learned where sin does abound, grace does much more abound!

Through my many mistakes, shortcomings, and backslidings, God chose me, as I was to become a vessel he could work through to see others saved. Today I pray someone who has failed God and who has heard the voices of the naysayers telling you that you cannot be used of God will be encouraged and know that God is not through with you yet!

Never allow the voices of negativity steer your vision and passion; I cannot tell you how many times I have been told I cannot, but God sent a victory every time by saying "I CAN"!

Table of Contents

Chapter 1 – Introduction

Chapter 2 – The Holy Ghost

Chapter 3 – Coming Back

Chapter 4 – Receiving the Revelation

Chapter 5 – When is a Soul Won?

Chapter 6 – Who Should Win Souls?

Chapter 7 – How to Win Souls

Chapter 8 – Where to Win Souls

Chapter 9 – Creating a Climate for Winning Souls

Chapter 10 – Don't Get Discouraged

Chapter 11 – Things to Avoid

Chapter 12 – Bus and Van Ministry

Chapter 13 – 10 Effective Ways to Win Souls

Chapter 14 – Closing Thoughts

Chapter 1

Introduction

My name is Tim Downs. I would like to share my story with you and also, by the end of this book, help you have a greater understanding of the greatest calling you will ever have in your life -- soul winning!

It has been a long journey over the last 45 years. I was born in 1965 in Northwest Indiana, and I have lived a very interesting life. My mother and father were divorced before I had my second birthday and most of my life was spent either without a father or with a stepfather that seemingly cared little about raising children.

My mother had three children; we are all one year apart in age. I have a younger sister and an older brother, making me the middle child.

At a very young age, my mother would often have us taken care of by an apostolic lady by the name of Hazel Plummer. I did not realize until much later in life that Sister Plummer was actually a next-door neighbor to my great grandmother Rena Jordan.

Introduction

My great grandmother was a great Saint of God who lived in Sullivan, Indiana. Sullivan is in the southern part of the state, just south of Terre Haute. Our family moved to Sullivan when I was 3 years old.

My great grandmother actually donated the land that the United Pentecostal Church in Sullivan, Indiana is located at now. Her home was across the street from the current church structure.

She lived for God until her passing in 1972.

During this time, Hazel Plummer babysat us and she would often try and teach us the things of God. Being such a young man, I really did not recall much of those teachings and at that time we didn't attend church very often if any.

I remember one afternoon when I was walking home from the city pool, I came across a lady walking to her mailbox. For some strange reason, this lady and I began a conversation. She invited me to church and told me if I wanted to go to heaven I would need to be baptized, and it would have to be in the name of the Father, Son and Holy Ghost.

After hearing this, I ran home and began telling Hazel about what this lady had told me. Hazel didn't waste any time; she began telling me that I needed to be baptized in Jesus' name and there was only one way to be saved! She handed me a gospel tract, told me to run back to the lady's house that I had met, give her the tract, and tell her that I had to be baptized in Jesus' name!

Introduction

Because I was so young, I obviously didn't know what I was doing. I just obeyed Hazel's command and did what I was told to do! Looking back now, I believe that was God using me in my first experience as a witness!

It was shortly after this incident that my life began to change. We moved away from Sullivan, which is a very small community, back to Northwest Indiana to a large city, Michigan City, Indiana. The people there were completely different than the small community that we had become accustomed to.

Michigan City, Indiana is located between Gary, Indiana and South Bend, Indiana; it is just 60 short miles away from Chicago, Illinois.

I began to hang around a crowd of kids who were always in trouble. These kids were continually in trouble by their parents, school principal, and the local authorities.

Because I was from a broken home, we were very poor. My mother did her best to support us; however, many times we struggled to have the basic necessities of life. We never had money to purchase the latest toys or clothes; we just barely had food on the table.

My mother did contact the apostolic church and have them begin to pick the three Downs kids up for church. My brother and I hated going, and we would do everything we could to get out of going to church. Most of the time we would get to the church and sneak out the basement doors to go hang out until the service was over.

Introduction

After a while, my mother never forced us to go anymore. In our minds, we were free!

Sadly, we had attended without ever learning much of the apostolic doctrine or teachings. It wouldn't be until many years later that I could look back on the opportunities I had to be a part of such a great movement, and each time I was lured away by the enemy of my soul.

I remember when I was 6 years old; a young boy from down the street from us was talking to me one afternoon about needing a bicycle. He was very insistent that I have a bicycle to join him and the other kids in their after-school activities.

Sadly, with my head hung low, I began to tell him, we didn't have the money to buy a bicycle. I remember it like it was yesterday. He slapped me on the back and said, "Don't worry, you don't need money to get a bicycle! We will get you one after school today. Meet me on the playground after the bell"!

"Wow," I thought, "this is awesome. I am going to get a bicycle and it's not going to cost me anything."

I could hardly wait for the school bell to ring, dreaming about the bicycle that I was going to get after school!

When the bell rang, I ran straight out to the playground, faster than I have in all my life! There my friend stood, right under the monkey bars, looking like he held in his hands the answers to every problem known to man!

Introduction

With excitement, he began laying out the plan: we were going to walk down the alley and he would explain more when we arrived at the location of the bicycle.

We walked a couple of blocks from the school and just a short distance from my home, he said, "Here we are." We stood outside of a garage, and he said, " Ok, grab the biggest rock you can find"!

I really don't remember thinking that what we were getting ready to do was wrong; it just seemed that in the moment of excitement I obeyed my friend's instructions and did what he said to do.

I grabbed a huge rock and he said, "Now, throw it through that window." I didn't think about it – Wham! I threw it right through the center of the glass and it left a huge hole where we could reach in and unlock the garage.

My friend then instructed me to grab the bicycle and ride as fast as I could back to the school as soon as he opened the garage door.

There I was-- the new owner of a stolen bicycle! In just a few moments, I went from a basically innocent young boy to an outright thief!

Looking back, I can see how the enemy of our soul does not wait until we are a teenagers or adults; he seeks to destroy us from the moment you are born!

That day proved to be a little incident that led me to a life of sin.

Introduction

It seemed that the older I got, the more sin I found. I remember at a very young age taking up the habit of smoking cigarettes, then from cigarettes to marijuana, then to cocaine and pills and alcohol.... a life of stealing and robbing and unthinkable crimes.

My life was a complete mess. I was so young and involved in so much wickedness. By the time I was 14, I was dependent on drugs and alcohol to get me through the day. I hated school. I don't have any idea how I ever got out of middle school; the only thing I can think of is the teachers didn't want me there anymore so they passed me to the ninth grade.

In the ninth grade, I think I attended school maybe two weeks, and then I found a new friend who loved to party as much as I did.

We would get to school on the bus and walk in the front doors and out the back to spend the day getting high and drunk and stealing to buy our next fix.

After just a couple of weeks, the teachers began to really come after me so I decided to drop out of school and never return.

Here I was, a young man with an eighth grade education, completely blinded to the enemy's plan to ruin my life.

After quitting school, life became much harder. We would spend days and nights getting high and staying out all night. I spent my time in and out of jail, breaking every law, and having no remorse for my wrong doings.

Introduction

Life was getting really bad for me. I moved to Chicago, living in the worst possible conditions, drugs, alcohol, and crime... every possible vice you could have imagined. I needed help!

When I was 19, I realized I needed help and I cried out to God. I didn't really know how to pray, but I did the best I could.

Not many days after praying and crying out to God, I ran into a young lady in Indiana whom I used to go to school with. She invited me to go to church with her in southeast Michigan.

At first I was hesitant. My sister went to the same church with this girl and I never really got along with my sister so I didn't want anything to do with it.

After a time of thinking, I decided to go with this young lady; after all she was pretty cute. Deep down I really figured I would get a date.

The day I went to the church, it was amazing, and I felt so much peace. The preacher was preaching right to me!

I remember getting out of my seat, walking to the old altar and in my own way crying out to God, asking for forgiveness! I remember being baptized in Jesus' name and receiving the Holy Ghost. Just as the Bible, when there were sounds as a rushing, mighty wind, I was filled with the Holy Ghost and I began shouting and speaking in tongues!

What a merciful God! He was able to forgive me of all of my sin; he washed me and made me new!

Chapter 2

The Holy Ghost

> *Our whole purpose on earth is to reach others, to share the gospel, to witness to every creature, to win the lost in every city. We shouldn't settle for less!*

The night I received the Holy Ghost, I was a new man. Just as John 3:5 declares, I was born again!

There I was, filled with the precious gift of the Holy Ghost! Words could not express how good it felt. Just like the Bible says, *it's joy unspeakable and full of glory*!

When I received the Holy Ghost, it was the real Holy Ghost. I know there are claims of a lot of different kinds of Holy Ghost experiences, but my experience was a true Biblical Holy Ghost experience!

A lot of people truly do not know that the Holy Ghost is not just given for a tongue-talking experience. According to scripture, speaking in tongues is the evidence of receiving the Holy Ghost. However, the purpose of the Holy Ghost was to give both power to become a witness and comfort!

Acts 1:8
But ye shall receive power, after that the Holy Ghost is come upon you: and ye shall be witnesses unto me both in Jerusalem, and in all Judaea, and in Samaria, and unto the uttermost part of the earth.

When I received the Holy Ghost, I received the tongue-talking, shouting, and dancing that also gave me the power to witness!

I want to spend a little time on this subject. I know that maybe it has been a while for some of you, maybe years since that wonderful day when God filled you with his spirit, but I will try and bring back something that maybe you have forgotten about that experience.

Maybe you can remember shortly after receiving the Holy Ghost, you were in a store, or at school, or on the job somewhere just minding your own business when all of a sudden you walked past someone and you heard this still small voice say, "Stop and talk to that person there."

It was the Holy Ghost speaking to you to witness to that person that you had just walked past. That was the power of the Holy Ghost in operation in your life!

At that moment, we had to make a decision about our obedience to God.

How did you respond? Did you obey the Lord and witness to that person and tell them how to obtain the salvation that you had been given?

The Holy Ghost

Sadly a lot of people resist the Holy Ghost and instead of witnessing to that person, they begin to make excuses like, *I cannot witness to them, I'm shy.* Or, *I cannot talk to them; they will make fun of me.* Or, *I cannot talk to them; they don't want to live for God.*

All of the sudden, we turn our back on the Holy Ghost and go about our business in life while leaving the lost to themselves.

Because the Holy Ghost is a gentleman, he will speak to you again, "Stop, talk to that lady in the isle next to you!" It may happen several times in your walk with God, as he is trying to get you to use that power that he has given you.

As many have done, they continue to make excuses until finally some day you no longer hear that voice compelling you to reach others.

Has this happened in your life? Have you resisted to the Holy Ghost so many times that you no longer feel that compassion towards a lost soul or until you no longer have a desire to reach a sinner with the wonderful gospel of Jesus Christ?

We must stir up that gift that is in us! We must have an awakening in our spirit that rises up and gives us a renewing and fresh calling to reach our neighbor!

Many churches today are deceived into believing that we are operating in our calling by showing up to service each week, paying our tithes, being obedient to the pastor, and keeping a standard of holiness.

This is a lie. Our whole purpose on earth is to reach others, to share the gospel, to witness to every creature, to win the lost in every city! We shouldn't settle for anything less.

I have been in many churches across this nation and world who have settled for just having "good church", while they have left their first love and call of reaching the lost to become satisfied with a few songs, a short message, a shout, and an altar call.

God forgive us! We must get back to doing what we are called to do!

God has given me an understanding to why churches have accepted the "good church" mentality and received the professional Pentecostal experience as the normal life for an apostolic believer.

I have been in altar services by the multitudes, and large gatherings of saints will stand and make crying sounds and even make faces that suggest sadness and sorrow without ever having a tear wetting their face. Often I will address one of the believers with this question, "What are you doing"?

They will mostly respond by asking what I mean. I will then say, "Are you crying"? And without hesitation, they will always say yes, to which I will respond by saying, "That's strange. I have never known anyone to truly cry without tears!"

You see, we have almost allowed church to become habitual experience, we know when to stand, when to sit, when to come to the altar, when to fake cry to make the pastor believe we are spiritual.

There is a great danger to this type of experience. When we resist the Holy Ghost and the reason it was given to us, then you have believers looking for replacements, and people begin fabricating things to replace the supernatural power of God.

Here is a question for you today: Have you ever heard anyone preach that the angels are rejoicing over one sinner that repents?

I have heard that all of my Christian life. It wasn't until recently my wife pointed something out to me about that statement.

You see the scripture does not say the "angels" are rejoicing over one sinner. It says:

Luke 15:10
Likewise, I say unto you, there is joy *in the presence* of the angels of God over one sinner that repenteth.

You see, the Bible does not say it's the angels rejoicing. Instead, it says there is joy in the presence of the angels! It is God himself that is getting the joy in the presence of angels! We know this to be true because the Bible declares, it's not his will that any should perish but all come to repentance!

I began to get a great revelation out of this, I began to understand why a lot of Christians come to church and do things out of habit many times without there being a true power or strength in their life to do the will of God.

Many of the people today in our churches are honestly weak and tired and worn down; they have very little, if any, strength to fight the good fight of faith.

The Holy Ghost

The reason why is because they have not compelled someone to repent of their sins in a very long time, if ever! You see when the Holy Ghost activates inside you, it tells you to reach for someone who is lost. It gives you power to witness to them and compel them to repent and be baptized so God can fill them with the Holy Ghost!

When we are obedient to God and the person we have witnessed to takes that step to repent, it gives God great joy in the presence of all the angels! In return, here is the revelation you need to get a hold of -- When we give God joy, he will give you something in return: strength.

For the joy of the LORD is your strength.

You will never have as much strength as you will when you are in God's will, reaching the lost, and bringing them to a place of repentance!

I remember the day the day I received the Holy Ghost I wanted to tell everybody I could about Jesus! Everywhere I went, I witnessed and tried to win souls.

I started winning souls right away! I couldn't find enough people to talk to about Jesus!

I remember not being so wise in my new walk with God, making a commitment to visit every Trinitarian church in our area. I wanted to ask to speak to the pastor to tell him they were on their way to hell unless they were baptized in Jesus' name!

I didn't have as much as wisdom as I did zeal in those days!

The Holy Ghost

I won several people to the Lord as a young Christian; I did my very best with as little knowledge as I had.

It wasn't long after getting into church that I fell into sin and backslid. I didn't have any discipleship as a young Christian, and I was basically just left on my own to learn what I could about God. Before I was truly rooted in the church and truth, my flesh became more important and soon I was allowing sin to rule my life.

That is why we must take time with these precious new converts and disciple them and love them until they can get roots in this wonderful truth!

Although I was involved in sin, I could not escape the presence of God. One thing about the Holy Ghost, it will never leave you or forsake you!

There I was back out in the world, living a life of sin again! Not one day went by that I didn't want to be back in church. Every day I would pray and ask God to help me get back in the church.

I could not face the people in the church, many of them wouldn't even talk to me anymore, and I heard a lot of the people were talking bad about me. I felt so terrible; I could hardly face them.

During this time, I learned something about being backslid. We must receive the backsliders back into our churches, and we must be the same example to them as the story of the prodigal son. His father never looked down his nose at him, he never gossiped about him, he greeted him with open arms and forgiveness and love!

There are millions of backsliders out there, and they want to come back, but they are afraid of how you will look at them. We must go to them, we must extend our hand to reach them and lift them up when they are down.

As a backslider, the Holy Ghost was still alive inside of me. I actually won more souls as a backslider than anyone in our church at that time.

The reason --God gave me the Holy Ghost and power!

I remember one night sitting in a bar with several of my friends. I was completely drunk and feeling no pain. After all my friends left, I remember sitting on the bar stool all alone.

All of the sudden I heard this young couple begin to argue and fight with each other. They were screaming and yelling at each other for the whole world to hear them. I thought they were going to either be kicked out of the bar or the police would arrive very soon and haul them off to jail.

All of the sudden while sitting there minding my own business, I heard the young lady tell the young man, "If we could just find a good church to go to, all of our problems would be over." Immediately, the Holy Ghost spoke to me and said, "Stop and go talk to them"!

I shook my head a couple times and spoke out to God; I said, "God, I cannot talk to them. I'm backslid and drunk!"

The Lord spoke again, "I said go talk to them"! Now, I'm no dummy. I am not going to resist the Holy Ghost. So, I got off my stool and walked quickly to the table where this young couple sat.

The Holy Ghost

I said, "Excuse me, I'm not trying to ease drop or listen to your conversation, but just now I just heard her say to you, if you could just find a good church to go to, your problems would be over. And I know I'm not living right myself, but I know the greatest church in this town that if you all want to go, I can take you next Sunday!"

They both looked up at me with tears in their eyes and said, "We would love to go to your church!"

That next Sunday, I drove over to their home and they were standing outside waiting. I picked them up and drove them to the church.

We walked in and sat down on the back seat. (That's where all backsliders and sinners sit when they go to church!) We sat there and began to listen to the songs and then the preaching, The Pastor didn't have any idea who these people were, and all of the sudden he closed his notes and began to preach on sin and how it destroys marriages and how God can put lives back together again!

It's amazing how God can speak through the pastor right to the hearts and situations in our lives!

All of the sudden, with tears flowing down their faces, the pastor said, "If you want a new life and want to receive the Holy Ghost and be forgiven of your sins, come down here to the altar and began to tell God you're sorry!"

I didn't have to ask them. They stood and we all walked down the aisle to the altar. In just a few moments they began to weep and cry and ask God's forgiveness. All of a sudden, they both received the gift of the Holy Ghost!

After they prayed a while, I told them they would have to be
baptized in Jesus' name. The Pastor shook my hand and
thanked me for bringing them. He said he would get them
baptized and make sure they had a ride home. He knew from
past experience when I had brought others I would just stay
until they were born again and then leave the service.

As I turned to walk out, I noticed not one person from the
church had gotten out of their seat to come and help us pray.
They all just sat there watching. As I was leaving, I had to
walk down the aisle past them. I could literally hear people
began to murmur things like, "Oh who does he think he is,
who are those people he is dragging in here, he isn't even
living for God himself."

It seemed by the time I was to the back of the church I could
even hear them growling and snarling! I thought, "Man I
have to get out of here!"

I am not saying this to be negative; I am saying it to make a
point. When backsliders come back into our churches, if all
they see is people looking down on them and bringing up
their past and showing no mercy, we will never get them
back!

We ought to go to them, hug them, and tell them how much
we miss them. We should spend time each day praying for
them and lifting them up before the Lord. The last thing a
prodigal should have to happen is another kick while they are
down.

Maybe as you are reading this book, you are realizing that you have not been obedient to the voice of God when he tells you to reach for a soul. I pray you will continue to read and allow me to help you learn effective ways to reach the lost and become a great witness for the Lord.

I believe you can become a great soul winner. You just need a little wisdom and an effective tool to become a life line to someone who is lost and in need of salvation!

Chapter 3

Coming Back

It's all right to shout in a restaurant! It's ok to shout in the grocery store! It's ok to praise God on your job! It's the right thing to do to worship Jesus at school! Don't ever let anyone put out your fire.

In my walk with God, it has often been a struggle to stay in the church living for God. I have failed him many times.

There is one thing I can say without hesitation. I love God with all of my heart, and I never wanted to fail him or backslide. Looking back today, there are several reasons I believe I struggled in staying faithful in the church.

Probably the most important reason is that I had never been taught anything about discipleship. I came out of the most horrid life of sin you could imagine, and now I was expected to live holy and measure up to people who have been born and raised in the church. I am writing about this to try and help churches realize that just because someone comes into the church, repents and is baptized, and is filled with the Holy Ghost, it does not mean they do not still have things that need to be changed in their life over time.

Coming Back

I remember the night I received the Holy Ghost a group of young people took me out for pizza to celebrate. As we were getting ready to eat, I being new to the church just grabbed a hold of the first piece of pizza and put it towards my mouth to take a bite. The young lady who invited me yelled out, "Stop!" I was confused. She then began to explain that it is important to always pray before we eat our food.

As she began to pray over the meal, I began to pray as well. All of a sudden, just like back at the church in the altar, the Holy Ghost came down in that restaurant and filled me again! I began to stand to my feet and speak in tongues and then I yelled out as loud as I could, "I just got the Holy Ghost again!"

You should have been there to see the looks on their faces. People began telling me, "Shhhh! We're not in church. Be quiet, you're going to embarrass us." One person even said, "We don't do that outside the church."

I found out years later who those people are. Today, we call them "fire extinguishers." About the time someone from your church catches the fire of the Holy Ghost and wants to act Apostolic, you will always have those around you trying to put out your fire!

I have good news! It's all right to shout in a restaurant! It's ok to shout in the grocery store! It's ok to praise God on your job! It's the right thing to do to worship Jesus at school! Don't ever let anyone put out your fire. Go tell everyone you meet about the King of Kings and the Lord of Lords!

After finishing our pizza that night, I walked to my car to go home. I remember getting into my car and reaching for my cigarettes. I had smoked since I was 11 or 12 years old, and I was addicted to tobacco.

I pulled one out and began to smoke without even thinking it was wrong. As a matter of fact, I smoked for at least two months after getting the Holy Ghost. The reason, well I received the Holy Ghost but I had not been delivered from all of my vices.

That's something we will have to learn to understand when reaching the lost. Many of them have grown up with some terrible things happening in their lives. Yes, sometimes God performs a miracle and delivers them in one night of all of that stuff. But in most cases, people still have all of those things to deal with after the new birth.

We cannot expect people who have lived a life of sin to come in our churches and act and look just like us when we have been in this for years. They are babies! We have to treat them and care for them as babies or they will never last!

We also have to be very careful in spending more time making people lovers of Pentecost more than lovers of God. I have seen it way too many times in our churches. As soon as a new convert comes in, there is someone there already trying to tell them how to dress, what they can do and shouldn't do. I am all for standards and holiness; however, if you teach someone how to fall in love with Jesus, he will teach them how to fall in love with holiness!

Coming Back

We also must be very careful that we do not choke the new converts out with too much Word in their beginning months of being in the church. I have seen it multitudes of times; as soon as a new convert comes in, there are people who want to get them in a home Bible study teaching them every doctrine known to man.

Give them the milk, let them grow for a while, love them, and baby them!

As I struggled to live for God, I was also missing something that was the most important ingredient to living for God and staying faithful.

I didn't realize what it was until the last time I came back to church. Pastor gave me something that changed my life forever... it was a prayer guide!

I learned a great deal about what prayer was, and what prayer was not. You see I never had a problem coming to prayer meeting, praying a while, and leaving. I just followed what I saw others doing, and to be honest, I basically walked around a dark sanctuary with one eye open and one eye shut saying things like "Oh, hallelujah" and "thank you Jesus" over and over again and once in a while asking God to give me things.

I didn't realize that was really truly not prayer. Prayer is a communication with the savior. It's a relationship, and to be true in prayer we have to be able to pray and then listen to what the Lord has to say back to us.

Coming Back

I know a lot of people who pray for hours, sometimes speaking the same things over and over and they never stop speaking their prayer long enough to hear what God has to say to them.

Communication is two-way! We must learn to pray and then just be quiet while the Lord speaks back to us. "My sheep will know my voice".

My Pastor gave me a prayer guide that outlines the different parts of prayer, such as praying for your family, church family, nation, city, leaders, pleading the blood, binding, and loosing things.

It is my belief that prayer is the number one thing that every believer will need to learn in order to stay in the church and have a close walk with God.

Every person reading this should seek to find a good prayer guide that can help outline the focus of things that you need to cover when praying.

In the Bible the apostles said to Jesus, "Lord, teach us to pray." You see, there is something we need to learn about prayer. It is more than just speaking a wish list to God.

I recommend at least one solid hour of prayer per day. If you use a prayer guide, it will be easy to pray at least an hour. If you are a new convert, maybe starting out with 15 minutes to 30 minutes will be good until you mature in God.

Coming Back

It was not easy coming back to church because I really felt bad for failing, I also had heard some of the people from the church speaking about my failures and to be honest, it hurt. For years I wanted to come back, but it was so hard to face some of the people who I just knew didn't want to see me come back.

I had to make up my mind that it did not matter what others wanted, I had to make it to heaven. I had no faith when I was backslid, and I knew if I were ever going to get back in church I would need to have faith. The only way I could figure out how to get faith without going to church was to watch it on the Internet.

For two solid years I used to watch the live Internet broadcast of Calvary Tabernacle Church in Indianapolis, Indiana with Pastor Paul Mooney. I never missed a service; I even tuned in to watch the special services they held.

It was a lifesaver for me. I am forever grateful for the vision of churches to broadcast their services for others to view.

After feeling like I had enough faith to come back to church, I made up my mind that nothing was going to stop me. One Sunday night I drove to the church, sat down on the back row (because that's where backsliders and sinners sit) and I listened as the Pastor began to preach. He spoke of forgiveness, God washing away all of your sins, and how much God loved us even though we failed.

I couldn't wait until he gave the altar call, and as soon as he asked everyone to stand, I walked down to the old altar, tears flooding my eyes. I knelt down and began crying out to God for forgiveness. It was in just a few minutes, God began to refill me with the Holy Ghost and I began to speak in tongues and magnify God.

That night something happened to me. As I began to thank God for forgiveness, I also made a commitment to God. I said, "Lord, since you forgave me, I want to make a commitment to be the greatest soul winner the world has ever known. I want to spend my life reaching others for you!"

I did not want to come back to church and just fill a spot. I did not come back to fill a position in the church. I came back to do the will of God and win every soul I can!

It's ok to make commitments like that. We need to set goals in our walk with God, not little goals but huge goals!

I have often heard of the "Everyone Win One" theory of church growth. I couldn't disagree more with a program to win the lost. The problem with that theory is that if someone's goal is to win one soul and they didn't do it, they didn't win anyone!

Why not say everyone wins 100 this year, and if someone shoots for that high of goal, chances are more than likely they are going to at least win some!

I spent a lot of time in prayer and God would speak things into my life like I was going to win 1,000 people in one year. I have to be honest, sometimes when God speaks huge things like that into your heart you have to hit yourself in the head a couple of times to make sure it was God!

Coming Back

After coming back to God, I did everything I could to pray and reach the lost. I had never been so close to God in my life. I truly believe that this was the first time I was actually living for God in my life.

I remember going to General Conference in Richmond, Virginia. (General Conference is the National conference for the United Pentecostal Church International.) I was so excited to hear the preaching of the Word; God was really dealing with me at that time.

I remember one night Brother David K. Bernard was preaching. He preached on soul winning and planting churches and reaching the lost. I was so impacted that I wept for over one hour!

After the service, I walked across the street to the Publishing House display. I had such a burden to learn more about soul winning and reaching the lost. I asked the young lady who waited on me to get me every soul-winning book she had in the store. I wanted to buy every one of them! She looked at me with a huge smile, she said, "yes sir, follow me and we will find them."

We began our search, table after table, box after box, looking for all of the soul winning books we could find. We looked around for almost 45 minutes searching every corner, and sadly we could not find one book that taught how to win souls!

Finally as I was leaving the display area, the young lady yelled and said, "Wait; there is one more place to look." I walked back and she reached inside of a box that was sitting on a truck, she pulled out a book called "Go Win Souls" by R. A. Russell.

I was really shocked; in all of the books that were at the display there was not one book that could teach me how to win souls! I purchased the "Go Win Souls" book and headed back to my hotel room. I was so hungry and so burdened that I read the entire book in just a few hours. The book did not really teach how to win souls but it did have some incredible testimonies on how Brother Russell won different people.

After reading the book, I fell to my knees and in a spirit of travail for several hours, I began to pray to God to help us learn more about soul winning and reaching the lost. I wanted to learn every method and every tool that was available.

During this time of prayer God spoke to me and said, "I want you to teach my people how to win souls!" God began to outline a plan to open a website and call it GOWINSOULS and on this website I could put all of the sermons on soul winning I could find, also I would write articles on soul winning and make available what tools I had already been using to reach the lost. He also made it clear that I would provide this to everyone for free.

I did not hesitate. The moment I arrived back home I began creating the website and searching for preaching messages on soul winning.

I must admit, I was shocked at the limited amount of sermons out there that was preached just on soul winning.

The majority of the messages I found in the beginning were from the Pentecostals of Alexandria. Pastor Mangun and his family had some incredible messages about reaching the lost. They have been a great inspiration to me, seeing the many souls that they have won and built such an incredible church.

I came across one message that would change my life, it was preached at the Because of the Times Conference in 2004 and it was entitled "Addicted to Soul Winning" by Brother Matt Maddix.

I believe that one message has been the turning point in the apostolic movement to get us back on course to winning the lost.

I began building and adding to the website as often as possible and it seemed without much effort the website began getting hundreds of hits and visitors. People started emailing me about how they could win souls too.

In just a short time of having the site online, I was already receiving between five to ten emails per day from people all over the world wanting to know more about souls winning!

The Lord laid it upon my heart to start writing a newsletter about soul winning, so I added a box that allowed people to enter their email address to receive a free newsletter.

I have written several articles on the subject of soul winning over the years. If you're interested in reading them, they are all available for free on our website www.gowinsouls.com. Simply click on the *download resources* button and then the *other materials* button.

Chapter 4

Receiving the Revelation

> You see, without a revelation of soul winning, we could be in great danger of being lost!

Several months after starting the website for Go Win Souls, I began to study more and more about soul winning in the Bible.

God was beginning to open my eyes to a great revelation of reaching the lost. The more I studied, the more I realized I had not known. There truly is a revelation of soul winning!

It all really began to happen one evening when I sat down to read a new book I had purchased. The book was by Charles Spurgeon; he is known to many as the world's greatest soul winner. I disagree with that position due to the fact that he, to my knowledge, was not born again of the water and the spirit and baptized in Jesus' name. Therefore, he could not be winning people if he was not giving them the truth about salvation.

As I began to read this book, I came across a quote that Mr. Spurgeon had made. He said this, "Have you no wish for others to be saved, than you are not saved yourself be sure of that."

Receiving the Revelation

When I read those words, I was immediately arrested in my spirit. I was shocked and honestly angry reading it. The reason why I was so angry is because I, truly in my heart, always felt that soul winning was important but I didn't believe if I never won others I would be lost myself.

When I read this, I felt angry because all I could think was, "Who does this guy think he is, telling me, an apostolic believer with the real truth, that I'm lost for not winning others? After all he is not saved himself as far as I can see!"

I became so angry and frustrated that I took my Bible, a Strong's concordance, a notebook, and three bottles of water in my room and decided to not come out until I proved this man wrong!

For three days, I studied the word of God and the subject of soul winning. The interesting thing was, every day I began seeing more and more how this man was right and I was wrong!

By the third day of my intense study, I walked out of that room with over 30 passages of scripture that clearly show we will not be saved ourselves if we neglect to be fruitful and win others.

I learned a lot of lessons about being a Christian that day. You see, to be honest, I have always thought that being born again of the water and the spirit with the understanding of the oneness was truly all we needed in our walk with God.

I was blinded in part, not knowing that God has way more for the body of believers than just one revelation that separates us from the rest of the religious world.

There are a lot of people out there that have a spiritual blindness; they have scales on their eyes so they cannot see certain things in the spiritual sense.

For instance, we have the revelation of the Oneness of the Godhead, but if I walked into a church that did not have that same revelation and told them that they must be baptized in Jesus' name to be saved, they no doubt would look me in the eye and say, "I don't think so; I know I am saved."

The reason why is they are blinded. They cannot see that they must be baptized in Jesus' name so they live their life for God in the false doctrine of the trinity.

They could not see that revelation; however, even though they were baptized in the trinity formula they were born of the spirit, being filled with the Holy Ghost and speaking in tongues, they believe that is essential to making it to heaven.

That same person could walk into another church that did not believe in speaking in tongues and tell them they could not make it to heaven unless they received the Holy Ghost with the evidence of speaking in tongues!

The person they spoke to would no doubt say, "Oh no, I know I'm going to heaven. My daddy's the Pastor and I know I'm saved!" You see they are blinded to the fact that they need to receive the Holy Ghost with the evidence of speaking in tongues!

Receiving the Revelation

Now this person can go to another church and find something that the believers of that congregation cannot see and tell them they cannot be saved as well.

Each group of believers cannot see something that they are missing out on; however, they can all see something that another group is missing in their walk with God. Even though they are blinded to something themselves, they are always able to see what others are missing out on.

This began to stir me. I began to ask God to search my heart – to find blindness in my heart and spirit.

Could it be possible that we, the apostolic believers, have the greatest revelation of all in the oneness of the Godhead, and we too have been blinded to revelations because we, like the others, have felt we had it all and were saved?

Pray and ask God to give you understanding. Always be open to study the word of God and to know assuredly that what you believe is true!

You see, without a revelation of soul winning we could be in great danger of being lost!

I have read in the scripture many details about the end time church and the warnings about earthquakes and people being lovers of pleasures more than lovers of God. Those things are really eye opening to me; I do not want to be blind to those things!

One of the things I fear we have overlooked is one of the reasons God has given us the Holy Ghost... that is to have power to become a witness!

40

There is also a place in the Bible that I believe goes along with this that we have to really consider.

2 Timothy 3:5
Having a form of godliness, but *denying the power* thereof: from such turn away.

I believe in most of our churches we have the *godliness* part down. We don't smoke, chew tobacco, or cuss. We dress modestly and have the holiness down, but have we really used the Holy Ghost power to become witnesses? Have we denied the power and left it laying at the altar in our Holy Ghost experience?

Could it be possible that we, as the apostolic group of believers, are missing a revelation in our own walk with God? Could it be possible that we are just as blind as others when it comes to missing out on a revelation, yet we, just like them, are certain that we have all we need?

Recently I posed the question to over 100 apostolic believers on an Oneness social media site. I asked the question, "Have you ever personally won a soul since living for God?"

To my surprise, after reading the results, only 2 out of the 100 people had ever personally won someone to God!

While preaching at the General Conference for an apostolic organization a couple of years ago in Los Angeles, California, I asked a question to a group of over 400 Oneness preachers who were gathered together that afternoon. I asked them to lift their hand if they had ever studied the subject of the Oneness of God.

Not surprisingly, every single person raised their hand, indicating that they had studied the subject of the Oneness of the Godhead. Then I asked the question to the same group, "How many here today would be real honest and raise your hand if you have ever personally studied the subject of soul winning in the Bible?"

I was truly shocked that only 2 people raised their hand and said they had studied the subject of soul winning in the Bible!

Could this be why we do not have the revelation? I truly believe that if every apostolic believer would study the subject of soul winning like we have the subject of the Oneness of the Godhead, we would turn our world upside down with the soul winning passion and desire to win others!

Would you make a commitment to God right now, that you will do your very best to study the subject of soul winning at least as much as you have studied the subject of the Oneness of the Godhead?

We always ask people to make a thirty day commitment to spend at least one hour per day for thirty days on our website www.gowinsouls.com listening to at least one preaching message on soul winning and reading at least one article on soul wining from our site.

I truly believe whatever we put in our spirit will come out of our spirit. If you listen, study, and read soul winning, you will become a soul winner!

You may also want to try and attend a Soul Winners Boot Camp that Brother Matt Maddix hosts all over the world. These Boot Camps can be a great start to getting inspired and trained to win and disciple souls to the Kingdom of God! You can learn more about the dates of the events on the soul winners Boot Camp website, www.swbootcampfire.com.

There are two books I recommend for any soul winner desiring to learn more or get inspired. They include "Keepers of God's Dream" by Joy Haney. You can purchase this book at www.pentecostalpublishing.com. The other is "Whose Child is This?" by Bill Wilson, available at www.metroministries.com.

Chapter 5

When is a Soul Won?

> *There is a difference between soul winning and discipleship. Soul winning happens in an instance, discipleship takes a lifetime.*

This seems to be the biggest misunderstanding of the whole subject. Many are completely blinded to knowing exactly when or how a soul is won. The reason again, is because most people have not studied the subject of soul winning. They just have a strong belief of what it is and without true knowledge of the subject, tend to speak their mind.

Have you ever heard of the old saying, "I never talk about politics or religion"? People make that statement because they have never studied the subject of politics, taken time to study the ins and outs of each party, and its beliefs. They have shaped their views about specific political parties because someone they were close to and trusted encouraged them to believe a certain way. The same thing is true about religion. Most people in the world today, believe it or not, have not studied the word of God. Yes, some have read it; some have studied portions, but in general, most have not actually studied the whole word of God.

When is a Soul Won?

People do, however, have very strong beliefs on what is right for salvation and making it to heaven. People believe certain ways because someone from their family, or close friend, or someone in their life that they trusted told them something and they accepted it without truly searching the word of God.

We must approach the subject of soul winning in the same careful manner. We must study to show ourselves approved. We must know for certain what the word of God says!

The Bible gives us a clear picture of when a soul is won. In the book of John, Jesus outlines the formula to being born again:

John 3:5

Jesus answered, Verily, verily, I say unto thee, Except a man be born of water and of the Spirit, he cannot enter into the kingdom of God.

When someone is born again, they become a new creature in Christ. They are purchased with a price, the blood of the lamb!

At the point someone is born again, that soul has been won to God.

A lot of people ask me the question, "Well, what if someone is born again one night and the next night they backslide? Are you saying that their soul has still been won?"

The answer is *yes*. Once a soul has been born, it cannot become un-born. When someone backslides, it does not negate the birth.

When is a Soul Won?

There is a difference between soul winning and discipleship. Soul winning happens in an instance, discipleship takes a lifetime.

When someone is born again of the water and the spirit, they are born again. Everything that happens after the new birth is discipleship and walking with the Lord.

We are not saved until we hear those wonderful words of our savior, "Well done."

Some people are won to the Lord and sadly after many years of living for God, they backslide. That doesn't mean that their soul was not won, it simply means they didn't endure until the end.

In order to win the lost and grow our churches, we must understand that we must reach the lost, we must win souls, and then we must disciple them.

I have heard it said many times, "Well bless God, what good is it to pray all those people through and baptize them if they are not going to stay?" Usually this is something of an excuse, meaning were not going to go win the lost because people don't stay.

The answer is not to neglect the harvest. The answer is we must win souls and disciple them!

When is a Soul Won?

I always ask the people who use that excuse some questions. I say, "By the way, out of all those who were baptized and prayed through, how many of them did you personally go visit? How many of them did you personally invite to your home for dinner? How many of them did you personally teach a Bible study too? How many did you personally call and make sure they had a ride to church?"

The answer is always the same: *NONE!*

We have to understand something about soul winning. When someone is born again, they become as a baby in the eyes of God. Spiritually they become newborn baby!

The statistics tell us, that if we brought a newborn baby home from the hospital and laid the child in a bed without touching, feeding, or caring for it in any way for three days, the child would not survive and it would die.

The same principle applies to spiritual babies. We cannot pray people through, baptize them in Jesus' name and send them on their way with a letter from the pastor thanking them for coming. We cannot expect them to survive!

We must get involved in their lives. We must personally make sure they are cared for, that they are notified of church services, that they have a ride, that they are visited and invited to our homes.

There is an old saying that says, "People don't care how much you know until they know how much you care!" We must love our new babies and protect them!

So basically it takes three things to win a soul:

1. We have to find someone who is lost and compel him or her to repent and be baptized in Jesus' name.

2. The person has to be willing to surrender to God. They have to be willing to make a new start and repent of their sins and be baptized in Jesus' name.

3. It takes a God with mercy to forgive them and fill them with the Holy Ghost. This is when the increase is given.

Once those three things are finished, we have personally won a soul.

Some people have made the statement, "Well, some plant and some water."

They say this suggesting that they just play a part in soul winning, and they do not personally ever win a soul.

This could not be further from the truth. It is a deception from the enemy to keep the people of God from wining the lost!

There are certainly times that we will plant seed, and other times when we will only water. But, we are instructed to go, compel, and persuade the lost. We must personally win souls.

When is a Soul Won?

For instance, let's say I am out on a soul-winning mission. I am looking for sinners to talk to and I come across a young man sitting on a bench. If I hand him an invitation to our church and he says he will try and make it sometime, did I win a soul? Of course not, I just planted a seed, he was not born again.

Another time I may see someone out at the mall. I begin talking to him or her and invite him or her to church. As I am speaking, they begin to cry and feel conviction, so I compel that person to come immediately to the church to repent and be baptized in Jesus' name. The person agrees to come. We take them to the church, we repent, we then baptize them and we ask God to fill them with the Holy Ghost. At this time, they did not receive the Holy Ghost. Did I win a soul? No, it takes being born again of the water and the spirit to be born again. God chose not to give the increase this time, so basically I only watered.

But sometimes we must win someone! There are many times when the person comes and repents, they are baptized, and God fills them with the Holy Ghost to give the increase!

Some people are deceived to believe that just because they are in a certain ministry in the church they are playing their part in soul winning. Therefore they are not required to go out and win the lost.

This is another form of deception. For instance, a lady who plays the music for the church claims she is a soul winner because she is the minister of music. Sorry, that is not soul winning. That is music ministry.

When is a Soul Won?

Someone says, "Well bless God, I am the Usher in the church. I do my part to win the lost by making sure there is order in the house of God." That is awesome, but that is not soul winning. That is ushering.

Someone might say, "Well bless God, I am a soul winner because I go out on outreach and hand out invitations. Well that as a great thing to do, but that is not soul winning. That is planting seed."

Someone says, "Well, I am a soul winner because I teach Bible studies to all the new converts. "Well, thank God for that ministry of teaching but that is not soul winning. That is teaching.

Someone said, "Well I am a soul winner because I am the pastor and I pastor all of these people." Well that is awesome and we need pastors, but the Bible tells us the five-fold ministry is for the perfecting of the *saints* not soul winning!

We absolutely need every one of the ministries listed above in our churches. They are very important; however, we cannot say they are soul winning when in reality they are given for discipleship.

Again, soul winning only happens when you personally go out and find someone who is lost and compel him or her to repent and be baptized and God gives the increase by filling him or her with the Holy Ghost!

If we can get this understanding, can you imagine how many more souls will be back in the fields of harvest seeking the lost?

When is a Soul Won?

I do not want one soul to be lost. I pray that each person reading this book will get a true understanding of soul winning and allow God to use you to reach multitudes of souls!

Everywhere you go there are lost people. All you have to do is take time with them, love them, listen to them, and compel them to repent and be baptized. In return, God is going to fill them with the Holy Ghost and give the increase.

We also must understand this to help solve a huge problem we face today with Holy Ghost Crusades. I am all for seeing every soul receive the gift of the Holy Ghost, but if that person speaks in tongues for ten hours and gets hit by a car without being baptized in Jesus' name, they have not been born again of the water and the spirit.

We must compel people to *both* be baptized and filled with the Holy Ghost!

Don't be afraid to compel them to be baptized. You may be surprised at how many will get in the tank right then! The Bible says there is no promise of tomorrow. We must do what we can to persuade people to be saved.

Chapter 6

Who Should Win Souls?

> *There is no ministry that exempts us from winning the lost.*

This is always a very serious subject. First let me say, I cannot imagine someone trying to wiggle their way out of winning others. Soul winners keep people from an eternal life of torment.

In Acts 1:8; the Bible proclaims we will receive a power to become witnesses. It does not give exclusions to anyone.

As a matter of fact, God is no respecter of persons. What one must do, we all must do.

One of the things that we will have to learn as leaders is that people will only follow you where you are willing to personally go. If you are not willing to win souls yourself, how do you expect people following you to win souls?

There is no ministry that exempts us from winning the lost. As a matter of fact our whole ministry should revolve around reaching the lost and the efforts to disciple people.

Who Should Win Souls?

When we received the Holy Ghost, God gave us a power to become witnesses. He instructed us to go and reach the lost. Once we receive a calling to a particular ministry, we cannot lay aside our main mission to reach the lost to focus on our ministry.

We must have a balance, and on one side of the scales it should be soul winning, personal evangelism, alone. On the other side of the scale should be everything else in your walk with God such as prayer, fasting, studying, ministry, etc....

A lot of people say to me, "You're out of balance with all your talk about soul winning." I often ask them, "If I'm out of balance with soul winning, when is the last time you personally won a soul? You're out of balance with ministry." We must maintain a balance of both.

Some people use the saying, "Well sheep begot sheep and because I'm a shepherd, I don't have to win souls, just the Saints need to!"

To be honest, this type of statement, in my mind, is almost blasphemous! How can we think we are exempt from reaching the lost because we have become a shepherd?

Jesus was the greatest shepherd of all yet, he gave his whole life to winning souls!

Also every pastor or shepherd I know also has a pastor in their life, which makes them a sheep as well!

Every person is called to ministry. When a person comes out of the water, they should be placed in some type of ministry. This will keep them active and on fire for God.

Who Should Win Souls?

One of the greatest ministries to get someone involved in as a new convert is soul winning. People who just come to the Lord have a fresh fire and want to tell everyone they know about their experience.

There is also no age limit exempting us from soul winning.

I hear a lot of times that a person is too young or too old to win souls. This is another deception of the enemy. If the enemy can keep us from winning the lost, he wins that many more souls to hell.

If you are old enough to receive the Holy Ghost, you are old enough to receive the power to become a witness!

Someone said, "Well bless God, what about the 92 –year-old elderly sister that can't get out in the streets to win souls, but she spends hours in prayer for people. Are you saying she is not a soul winner?" Sadly *yes*, she is not winning souls by praying. She is doing an awesome job in that calling; however, there is no exemption for people to avoid winning souls.

We need the elderly to pray for souls, but they also must be active in winning souls. As a matter of fact, sometimes the elderly can be more effective at winning the lost than anyone else.

For instance, do you remember going to your grandma's house as a child? Maybe you were there with your mother and when you did something wrong your mother threatened to spank you or correct you. Just in time, grandma stepped in and said, "You're not spanking that baby at my house!"

Who Should Win Souls?

There is something about a grandma or grandpa figure in our life that expresses mercy. No matter how mean a person is, usually when they are approached by an elderly figure, they tend to calm down.

I understand this is not 100 percent of the time, but for the most part it is accurate.

So when a grandma approaches a sinner and asks them to repent, usually that person will be more than willing to listen and obey.

Also, a lot of older people were brought up in the era of the church when outreach and soul winning were more common. A lot of these elderly people, believe it or not, want to get back in the fields of harvest!

Children are the same. If we are ever going to reach this world, we are going to have to train up this next generation of children to win souls.

We cannot afford to place our children in segregated classrooms and keep them from sinners, teaching them to shun people who are lost. We must get our kids out of the play land and into the streets to win the lost.

You would be surprised to know how effective a child can be at witnessing and winning the lost. It's very hard for someone who would normally reject an adult to reject a sweet little child!

I have watched for many years; mothers of church children guard them and protect them from people just because they are sinners! We must teach our children to love the lost and reach for every soul!

Who Should Win Souls?

Another huge mistake, in my opinion, is putting our children in private schools and keeping them from children who are lost. How are we ever going to shine our light into the dark world if everyone around us is supposedly saved?

In most cases when I find someone who has never won a soul since being born again, they tell me the reason is because they are scared, they are shy, or they just fear the rejection of someone telling them no.

The last excuse is probably the number one excuse I hear. People who are making that excuse truly don't know what they're saying. You see, the Bible tells us that God has not given us a spirit of fear! The enemy of our soul gives you that spirit so you operate in bondage, preventing you from reaching the lost.

The enemy gives people the spirit of fear. It is no different than an addiction to drugs and it is a bondage that shackles people to sin. You might say, "Well, I'm not sure it's sin." The Bible says, "He that knows to do good and does it not." It is sin!

You see, when the enemy gives you that spirit, you are held hostage to the spirit of fear, never doing God's will, reaching the lost. The enemy actually wins.

You have to be delivered from that spirit the same way someone who is held captive to drugs or alcohol is delivered! God is ready to deliver you today. Be honest with him and he will set you free!

Again, how can someone with the Holy Ghost want to avoid winning others from the eternal damnation of hell?

For every person you reach, that's one more person that does not have to spend eternity in a lake of fire with eternal torment!

Pray and ask God to give you a fresh passion for souls! Ask him to lead you to the lost in your city! The fields are white! Will you respond?

Chapter 7

How to Win Souls

> *If what you are doing is producing no fruit, then don't just keep doing the same thing, find something that works!*

There are probably millions of ways to win souls; there is no one method to winning people. Yes, there are millions of ways to win souls, but there is only one way that a soul is born into the kingdom. He or she will become born again of the water and spirit as a result to your efforts. Each person will also bring in different amounts, like the story in the Bible:

But other fell into good ground, and brought forth fruit, some an hundredfold, some sixtyfold, some thirtyfold.

Although every person brought in different amounts, no one brought zero! Everyone contributed. Some people win people by teaching Bibles studies, while some win people by first becoming their friend, and then compelling them to repent and be baptized.

How to Win Souls

We are going to list 10 effective ways to win souls in another chapter. However, I want to cover a couple of things here to help you in winning the lost.

Several years ago I didn't know much about winning souls. I just did whatever came to mind, and most of the time those things were not very effective. For instance, when I made a commitment to go to all of the Trinitarian pastors in my area and tell them they were all going to hell if they didn't get baptized in Jesus name, guess how many I won? You got it, zero!

Whatever your method of soul winning is, make sure you are actually winning people to God. If what you are doing is producing no fruit, then don't just keep doing the same thing, find something that works!

I have tried a lot of things that did not work. I could have just hung my head and quit, but souls are way too important to just give up on. We have to reach them!

Be honest with yourself, look around your church, how many souls did you personally go out into the fields and find and compel them to repent and be baptized in Jesus' name? If there are none or just a few, we cannot be satisfied. Soul winning has no place of contentment, and we must not stop until every soul is won!

One way we have found extremely effective to win the lost is the "Heaven or Hell" method.

Heaven or Hell Method
(See a reproducible, printable script on page 123).

(The soul winner approaches someone and hands them a card or flyer and asks them if they're busy....)

<u>Soul winner</u>: Do you have one of these flyers? Are you busy right now?

<u>Individual</u>: No, I don't have one.

<u>Soul Winner</u>: Do you want to go to heaven or hell?

<u>Individual</u>: Heaven
(Soul winner waits for answer, and 99 times out of 100 the individual will say heaven.)

<u>Soul winner</u>: That's awesome! That's where everyone should want to go! Everyone says heaven but most people never do what it takes to get there. Are you sure you want to go to heaven?

<u>Individual</u>: Yes, I'm sure. I want to go to heaven.

<u>Soul winner</u>: John 3:5 says, "Except a man be born again of the water and the spirit you cannot enter the kingdom of heaven." Say CANNOT for me."

<u>Individual</u>: Cannot

<u>Soul winner</u>: It takes about five minutes to repent, and 10 minutes to be baptized the right way so God can fill you with the Holy Ghost. What would stop you from coming to do those two things right now?
(Most of the time the individual will answer by saying, either nothing, or that they have already been baptized.)

(When a person tells you they have already been baptized, the normal thing for apostolic people to do is ask them if it was in Jesus name and when they say "no", we start beating them over the head with our Bible and scriptures telling them how they will go to hell being baptized that way!)

60

Here is the way to handle it....

Soul winner: Oh, you were baptized already? Do you
remember if they said in the name of the
father, son and Holy Ghost, or Holy Spirit?
*(Most people have no idea what they said and whatever you
ask them, they will agree to it. That's why we never ask them
if they were baptized in Jesus name, because most people will
just say "yes." Then what do you do with them? If they say
yes to father, son and Holy Ghost, do not get out your Bible
and tell them how they are going to hell.
Give them a big high five.)*
Soul winner: Awesome! I have some good news and some bad
news. The bad news is that you weren't
baptized the right way. The good news is that
you can get baptized right now the right way so
you can go to heaven. What would stop you
tonight from being baptized the right way?

*(Most of the time they will say nothing will stop them, so you
tell them you have a church down the road, you have clothes
so they do not get their clothes wet, and you have water to
baptize them the right way. Continue asking them what
would stop them from coming right now.)*

You will be shocked to see how many people get in your
vehicle and come to the church to repent and be baptized! Do
you know why they do it? Because they are hungry for God
and want to go to heaven, but many times no one ever
compels them! In the last five years, our family, through the
GO WIN SOULS ministry, has baptized well over 12,000
people in Jesus' name and God has filled most of them with
the Holy Ghost. This method is probably one of the fastest,
most effective ways right now to win the lost.

Maybe it's not for you, maybe you could never do it, but you will never know until you try!

We also teach people that if they will do the "Heaven or Hell" method with guests in the church, 95 percent of the people who are asked in the pews will kneel down right there and repent and be baptized in Jesus' name! Why let people leave our churches without being born again?

We have baptized our restaurant servers, public servants, people at grocery stores, gas stations, skating parks, funerals, weddings, singles' retreats, block parties, home fellowship groups, and tons of other events. All you have to do is learn the method and try it!

The Bible declares, "In all labor there is profit." One thing about winning the lost, its work! When you're willing to work, God is willing to give the increase!

Whatever way you can win souls, use it to the best of your ability. Fill up your church with sinners and watch God's blessings being placed upon you!

There is no greater feeling than to win someone to God. Don't be discouraged. Find people who are winning others and ask their advice. You can do it!

Block Parties and Give Aways

Another great way to win souls is to try and fill up your church or location with as many souls as possible to expose them to an apostolic service. Then, have several people ready to compel those who attend to repent and be baptized so God can fill them with the Holy Ghost.

Block Parties and Give Away events generate thousands of
people. We have actually ministered to over 100,000 people in
the last 5 years, all first time guests. The only way that can
happen is if you're willing to go out and sow the seed and
offer them a reason to come and experience your service.

Some negative people say that those guests are just coming
for the gifts. Never let the negative people drive your vision.
Find positive people that believe in what you're doing and
will support you! If someone just came for a gift, it doesn't
matter! They were exposed to an apostolic service and they
will never forget what they felt!

Caring for Babies

We recommend having large gatherings of people at least
every quarter, bringing in as many as you can and then
spending the next three months retaining and teaching
discipleship classes to the ones you were able to reach. I truly
believe if you and your church will work hard at loving and
ministering to these new converts both in the church and out,
you will fill your church up in no time with the most loving
amazing people you have ever known!

We have a theory. You see in most cases, in any given church,
there are possibly only one or two people actually winning
souls as described in this book. Therefore, the babies are
seldom cared for like they should be.

In the long run, many do not stay. The reason this happens
is due to something we call the "nursery syndrome." You see,
going into a nursery and looking at all the beautiful babies is
actually pretty exciting for the first few minutes, but it
doesn't take long for the reality of caring for a baby to sit in.

Not many of the saints want to work in the nursery, it's hard work!

The same thing in the spiritual sense happens. You have one or two people winning souls or spiritual babies and they are often burned out quickly trying to care for them all.

The natural instinct of any mother is to care for her child. No one has to go home with a new mother and tell her to feed her child, to change her child's diaper, or to love her baby. Those things all come natural.

The same thing happens in the spiritual. If we could train every person in our church to personally win souls, or become spiritual mothers, we wouldn't have to worry about one or two people getting burned out trying to care for them all. Each mother would take care of her on naturally!

You can watch a video of the "Heaven or Hell" method on our website, www.gowinsouls.com, and also download the dialogue in English or Spanish.

We recommend learning it word for word and practicing it a few times before trying it.

Once you have learned how to overcome people's objectives, you will become a great soul winner!

Chapter 8

Where to Win Souls

Some claim they do not want to be in the rough neighborhoods because they do not feel safe. How will these lost souls ever see the light if the people with the light take it and hide it?

Everywhere you go, you should be looking for an opportunity to win someone to God. The fields are white. There are so many souls ready to come, that there are not enough soul winners to get them all!

The key to winning and being sensitive to souls is praying. Ask God before you leave your home or church. "Lord, lead me right to the hungry person you want to save today."

Almost every time I pray that prayer, God leads me to someone that is hungry and hurting and needing God!

When you are out, you can even tell the person you approach, "Listen, before I left my home I prayed and asked God to send me right to the person he wanted to save today, and guess where God sent me to out of all the people in this city? That's right, that's how much God loves you, and he sent me right to you!"

Where to Win Souls

Everywhere we go is a mission field; there are people in every direction that need God.

Restaurants are a great place to win souls. I cannot tell you how many of our servers we have won, just by being nice to them and leaving them a generous tip! Schools are another place for young people to win their friends and classmates. Believe it or not, young people are truly looking for God! Don't let this opportunity pass you by!

Church events and services are a great place to win souls. Find the new guests and go to them and compel them. The people who come to church are looking for more than a night of entertainment. Laundry mats are another great place to reach people because usually the people doing laundry have plenty of time to listen to what you say!

One of the things we have learned in reaching the lost is that just as in the days of Jesus, the hungry are the poor, blind, captive, broken-hearted, and hurting people.
It could be possible that we are not winning the lost because we are selecting whom we want to win instead of who is ready to be won. Sometimes we hear people boasting of how they invited their lawyer or doctor to church, putting a star trophy on the wall. That doctor or lawyer may never attend, while we ignore the ten poor people already on the pews who are starving for a touch of God.

If we neglect the poor and hurting people of our cities, we are neglecting the biggest part of the harvest. People rarely come to God when everything is going good in their life.

We have upgraded our churches in the bad neighborhoods to multi-million dollar facilities to entertain the church people while leaving the lost to a life of sin without hope.

Some of our churches are so nice, sinners feel uncomfortable and the lost have no transportation to get there. We almost make it impossible sometimes to reach the lost by our desires to fit in with the mainstream churches.

Some claim they do not want to be in the rough neighborhoods because they do not feel safe. How will these lost souls ever see the light if the people with the light take it and hide it?

If you move your church to a multi-million dollar facility, at least start a daughter work in the poor areas of town so those souls have somewhere to attend and be ministered too.

Most people do not attend church because they have no way to get there. Why not start church plants in every area of the city so people can walk to church!

I always have said that there would not be bad neighbor hoods if the enemy of our souls had not tricked us into the spirit of fear, believing we were in danger. Had the church not been afraid, we could have been bringing the people of the bad neighborhoods to Sunday School over the last 20 years and they would have grown up with a passion for God!

This is probably the hardest chapter for me to write, I just want to stay everywhere and end it! I don't think I can think of one place where you cannot or should not try and win souls!

Chapter 9

Creating an Atmosphere to Win Souls

> *Make sure you have friendly greeters. I cannot tell you how many times I have walked through the doors of a church to meet someone who looks and acts like they want to stuff me in a box and kill me.*

This is a very important part of soul winning. We must make it easy to reach the lost. We must create a positive atmosphere in our churches to reach souls and an atmosphere outside the church where we are compelled to reach others.

On the inside, we must realize that people who come to our churches are truly hungry for God. We must make every attempt to reach them and not let them leave lost.

Sometimes this means we only have one opportunity to reach them, so inside our churches we need to have an atmosphere of revival and love for souls.

Church studies conclude that someone makes up their minds with the first five minutes of visiting our churches whether or not they will ever return. What happens in your church that guests see when they first arrive?

Creating an Atmosphere to Win Souls

Many times the vestibule seems to be the place for kids to congregate, creating horseplay and confusion as kids do what they do best. Obviously kids will be kids, and we want them to enjoy church, so it's wise to make sure and have a friendly usher standing by to keep the peace.

If the kids are gathering out in the vestibule, find an alternative place for them to hang out. The last thing you need is for a first time guest to get struck in the head with a Nerf football.

Also you will want to try and make sure your sanctuary lights are bright and you have some exciting music playing. No funeral music or rock guitars, just a jazz style. Upbeat black gospel music is the best.

Make sure your pre-service prayer is not in the main area of the church. For instance, most churches have prayer 15 minutes before service in the sanctuary with the lights turned down low, funeral music playing, people marching around speaking in foreign languages, beating on the walls, wailing, and crying. Not the best way for new converts to come into the church!

People who know nothing about our style of worship get a little freaked out with all of that stuff. I'm not saying to give up pre-service prayer; I'm saying to find a location away from the front area of the church or sanctuary to have it.

Creating an Atmosphere to Win Souls

One of the worst places to move your prayer is on the other side of a wall in the sanctuary or in a basement right below the floor of the sanctuary. Can you imagine the thoughts of a first time guest who came in and hears all kinds of wailing and beating on the walls or floor and people speaking in different languages? You got it. Don't expect them to return.

We have to use wisdom in our services. We have to make services guest-friendly.

One of the other things that must be addressed is our style of music. If we are going to reach sinners, we must not play all traditional Pentecostal or new-style church music. We must mix in old songs like *Amazing Grace, Jesus on the Mainline,* and *I'll Fly Away.*

Sinners will be able to worship with those songs because most sinners can relate to them. Grandma, or someone important in their life, used to sing those songs!

Mix up your music culturally. Play some black gospel, some Hispanic, some new and old.

Make sure you have friendly greeters! I cannot tell you how many times I have walked through the doors of a church to meet someone who looks and acts like they want to stuff me in a box and kill me!

Make sure there is close parking for the guests. The Pastor should not have the best parking spot in the church. Ask the saints to always leave the front row open for guests.

Creating an Atmosphere to Win Souls

Sunday School should not be taught by people just filling positions. Find people with a passion and love for children. Use people who have creative minds and can make Sunday school fun and exciting!

Every church should consider this next suggestion.

Your Sunday services should be at 2 pm in the afternoon!

Here's why:

1. Sinners stay out all night partying on Saturday night; they are not going to get up at 9 am so they can be at your service at 10 am. Even if they didn't party all night, they most likely stayed up watching television or movies.

2. All the churches in your city probably have church at the same time as you on Sunday, an early morning service and late evening service. If you ever want to reach those people, you need to have an option for them to attend when they are not having service.

3. This is the most important reason of all. If you do not use this portion of the advice, don't bother with changing times. Everyone that is a member from your church should be instructed to meet together at the church at 11 am – 1 pm every Sunday and pick up flyers and cards and go out into the highways and byways compelling people to come to the 2 pm service. People will come more the day of the service than any other time you invite them.

Creating an Atmosphere to Win Souls

If there was one thing I could point to in churches that I see tremendous growth in, it is this suggestion of 2 pm service. Even if you can adjust your church to three services, make sure you have a 2 pm service.

Once guests arrive:

1. Make sure your church is clean and free of clutter. If you personally have issues with keeping stuff clean, appoint someone who has a very clean home. Ask them to tidy things up.

2. Make sure the restrooms are clean, paper and towels full, hand soap, and cleaners full.

3. Make sure the windows to the entrance of your building are clean and streak free.

4. Make sure the parking lot is not littered with garbage and the yard and premises are not littered with tools, machinery, trash and unnecessary items.

5. If you have a church sign, make sure it is well lit. Make sure the letters and information are correct.

6. Make sure you have music and choir practice way before service starts. There is nothing worse than coming to church, sitting through choir and music practice and then ten minutes later when the songs are sung; they are supposed to be spiritual.

7. Make sure your church vans and busses are clean, parked in straight lines, and filled with fuel.

Chapter 10

Don't Get Discouraged

> *We must fight the spirit, not the people! Love everyone, even those who talk about you! Pray for those who speak against you...love them even more!*

Galatians 6:9
"And let us not be weary in well doing: for in due season we shall reap, if we faint not."
I have wondered at times why anyone would become weary in well doing. As I became more passionate about souls and reaching the lost, I have learned to understand more about this scripture.

One would think, as life tells us, that good things happen to those who do good. We should consider, though, that we are working in the spiritual realm. We are fighting devils and pulling people from hell! We are fighting an enemy that is terrible in every way. He is out to steal, kill and destroy us! I have talked to other soul winners and heard many stories of some terrible things that happen in the lives of soul winners. We must be careful to not become weary in well doing! We shall come against fierce opposition.

73

The enemy of our souls will use unexpected people to talk about you, plot against you, and even try and cause you physical harm! I don't want to cause anyone to become alarmed, but listen-- soul winning is not the easiest job on this earth!

We must always remember that our reward will be in heaven! Sure, we will rejoice with sinners as they pray through, but we shall also fight battles for their souls!

People will feel convicted. Many people are not doing what they need for God, so when they see you reaching souls they have to get you down to their level. Many will gossip, lie, and cause you many unpleasant times. We must keep a good spirit and not react in a negative way. The devil is waiting for you to get angry and say something mean to someone so he can try and beat you down with guilt and shame and slow your work down. Do not be ignorant to the devils devices!

The Bible does not leave us powerless over these attacks.

Ephesians 6:12
"For we wrestle not against flesh and blood, but against principalities, against powers, against the rulers of the darkness of this world, against spiritual wickedness in high places."

Don't Get Discouraged

We must fight the spirit, not the people! Love everyone, even those who talk about you! Pray for those who speak against you...love them even more! Keep a good attitude, do not argue and get angry over anything people will do. One way to that will help you is to keep your weapons sharp! Pray and fast often, read the word of God, praise God and worship him during the trials. I know it will be hard to do, but this is the way the scriptures teach us to do battle! The weapons of our warfare are not carnal!

This means we do not attack our brothers and sisters! We must pray even more for them!

...THEY ARE NOT CLOSE ENOUGH TO THE FIRE TO PULL ANYONE ELSE OUT.

Don't Get Discouraged

One other thing that is so important to a soul winner's success is to stay in touch with other soul winners. We are in this together, and many have fought similar battles! We need each other! Learn to gain strength from your fellow soldiers! When we are down, we need to be lifted up through the love and compassion of our brothers and sisters. Take time to encourage people who are soul winners. Go out of your way to bless them. You never know what they may be going through!

We can make a difference in our world! We can bring souls out of the lake of fire! The price is not cheap, but the blessings are not worthless! Reach your community. Go with passion. Love your neighbor as yourself! The Bible is clear, we must reach the lost. If you are working to reach souls, you are in the will of God! Keep working, keep reaching, the last part of the scripture is our promise, "for in due season we shall reap, if we faint not."

Chapter 11

Things to Avoid

We are suggesting there are more effective ways, based on time and energy, to bring the largest harvest into the kingdom of God.

After many years of reaching the lost, I have learned some very valuable lessons. Those lessons were taught from the school of hard knocks, as we call it!

Just as I have learned some of the most incredibly successful ways to win the lost, I had also learned some of the worst ways to try and win others. I want to take a little time and try and save you some headaches by sharing those with you.

First of all we want to say, as in anything, if you do enough of it there will be some type of good result to it. What I am trying to do is help people get the best results possible in the shortest length of time. We have a huge job ahead of us if we are going to reach 6.5 billion souls.

Mistake 1: Debate and Bitterness

In my early soul winning days, I have already mentioned that I made a commitment to go to all of the Trinitarian pastors in our area and tell them how they needed to get baptized in Jesus' name or they were going to go to hell. Well this didn't work out too well. As a matter of fact, I didn't baptized even one of them!

I spent a whole lot of time in my early days just debating with people, trying to prove that we had the truth and they did not.

I really believe one of the greatest mistakes we have made after getting the revelation of oneness is allowing bitterness to grow in our hearts towards people who believe the Trinitarian doctrine.

This bitterness has caused us to become distracted from our mission of reaching the lost. You see, we have spent countless years debating with people over the issues of the Godhead, trying to prove them wrong and us right while neglecting the true hungry souls who were left out of the harvest.

I believe in oneness more than anything else; however, I have *never* won a soul through debate! I have won a lot of debates in my life, over the subject of the oneness, but I have never won a soul after winning the debate.

In many cases I have seen, oneness people immediately began to challenge the belief of another person and in just a few minutes it turns into a heated argument, winning no souls.

We must be very careful not to waste our time arguing with people. It has little or no results, and it usually makes more enemies than friends.

One of the best ways to avoid these debates is by not asking people up front if they are baptized in Jesus' name.

Things to Avoid

From the over 12,000 people who were baptized in the last five years, I would say that at least sixty percent of them had been baptized previously in the Trinitarian formula of baptism.

We didn't debate with them. We didn't argue with them. We just loved them and gave them the answer of how to do it the scriptural way.

Most people who were baptized the wrong way have no clue on what was said to them while being baptized. For instance, when someone is baptized in the name of the Father, Son and Holy Ghost there is little if any importance placed on the words spoken. So most people have no idea what was even said.

We have found that when approaching someone that has already been baptized the Trinitarian way, one should never ask if they were baptized in Jesus' name. One should always ask if they were baptized in the name of the Father, Son and Holy Ghost. This way they will most likely say yes, and it will be a positive approach. No one wants to be told they are wrong.

If you ask them if it was in the name of Jesus, and they don't really know, they will just say, "Yes, it was in Jesus' name." Whatever you suggest or say in the beginning, they will most likely just agree with it because there was no importance placed on that name.

Things to Avoid

Now if you ask someone that had truly been baptized in Jesus' name if they were baptized in the name of the Father, Son and Holy Ghost, they are going to stop you and say, "No, I was baptized in Jesus' name." The reason why is because people who are baptized in Jesus' name know why they are baptized that way!

So, when we come across someone that has been baptized before, we don't get into an argument with him or her. We don't hit them in the head with our Bibles as we scream Acts 2:38 in their ears. We simply say, "Were you baptized in the name of the Father, Son and Holy Ghost?" When they say *yes*, we give them five and say, "We have some good news and some bad news, the bad news is that no place in the Bible was anyone baptized the way you were, the good news is that you can be baptized the right way right now and it only takes about ten minutes to do it the right way"!

Then we say, "What would stop you from doing it the right way right now"? Usually the answer is, "Nothing would stop me!"

Once in a while they may ask what the right way is. I reply, "What is the name of the guy who lay on the cross and died for you?" When they say, "Jesus," I ask, "What did you say it was?" And when they say it again, I say, "That's right. That's the name you have to be baptized in. Now, what would stop you from doing it right now?"

Once they agree to be re-baptized it's very important to not talk about it anymore until after they are at the church and in the water. When they repent and change clothes and are sitting in the baptismal tank, I teach them about why it's so important to be baptized in Jesus' name. And I stress to them to never forget that precious name that they were baptized into.

In summary, never get into debates and arguments. There is an old saying that says, "People don't care how much you know until they know how much you care." Love them and be kind and gentle. You will win them!

Mistake 2: Door Knocking

The next thing that we must address is door knocking. Now again, I do know of some people who have had some success in the past with knocking doors, and I'm not saying it never works. I am simply promoting more effective ways.

I personally have never won a soul by knocking on a door. Every time I have tried, it has brought negative results and discouragement. As a matter of fact, people always tell me in my travels that when they hear we are going to do outreach, they already start making excuses because they were so worried we would be knocking doors.

Several different religious groups have brought a bad light to the old fashioned method of knocking doors. People do not want to be bothered in their homes. It is a place of privacy and security. When we go out and knock on people's doors, and the homeowner gets angry or says cruel things to us, it builds fear of rejection. Then, people will not want to participate.

In our experience, we have found that door hangers are much more effective. We use a bright, yellow door hanger with black ink to keep it very simple. When people see this on their door, it resembles a utility shut-off notice, so they are sure to retrieve it!

81

Some door hangers are too colorful and elaborate. We used them a few years ago and found they were very expensive and not as effective. People knew from all the fancy pictures that it was something we were trying to sell.

The other key to door hangers is keeping the religious wording off of them. For instance, you don't want to use words such as *Holy Ghost Crusade, Acts 2:38, Jesus' name, miracles, church,* or *Pentecostal.*

People in the world, believe it or not, are not interested in another church. In most cases, they have their own church. Even if they never personally ever attended a church, they still claim they have one. It's the one that grandma, or their mother, or someone they revere attends.

When trying to get people to visit, we must use something like a special event...a reason for them to come! We use the terminology, "blessing the community through giving". We have filled up churches all across the world using this type of wording.

Now, some people will say, "Well, they're just coming for the free stuff." I say, "Who cares why they are coming, we want them to hear the Gospel!" There is no difference in spending $300 on some prizes than spending $500 on a yellow page ad, or $1,500 on a billboard. Each enticement is serving the same purpose, to fill up the church with sinners!

Door hangers are very inexpensive. You can purchase 5,000 door hangers for around $212 printed and shipped! A great resource is Top Value Printing in Destin, Florida. Their website is www.topvalueprinting.com.

Things to Avoid

Mistake 3: Misplaced Spending on Advertising

While we are on this subject, let me try and carefully help you understand that you also must be cautious of spending thousands of dollars on billboards and television commercials. For the amount of money spent, you can reach thousands more souls using tools like door hangers and block parties.

I have owned several businesses in my life. I remember being lured into a marketing plan of having three billboards and 30 commercial spots a week on a major television network. The selling points were, the signs were going to be seen by millions of people passing by the most strategic locations in town, and the commercials would be aired on the most watched programs and time slots available.

The young lady explained that there would be 50,000 people per day who would see my advertisement! Wow! I was excited; I signed up that day and paid $4,000 without blinking an eye!

Well, three months went by and we kept detailed records, asking every customer how they had heard about our business. And to our surprise, not one customer in three months came from either the sign or the commercial.

While out in public, we did have a lot of people comment about how nice our signs looked and how much they liked our commercials. But these were people knew we existed and would have frequented our business anyway.

Use your money wisely and do what is most effective. Make sure you have a place on your guest cards asking how they found out about your church, or how they ended up coming to your church. In the end, it will save you thousands of dollars!

A lot of people have purchased bottled water as a form of outreach with the church name printed on the labels. While this is a nice gesture, it is very seldom effective as an outreach method. Again, we are not saying it's impossible for someone to come as a result of this. We are seeking to help you evaluate this method. If you spend $1,000 on bottles of water and get one or two people to visit one time, was it really worth it?

This method is not effective because once someone drinks the water, they discard the bottle. They do not sit and peel off the label, stick it in their pocket, and make a commitment to attend your church. They drink the water and throw away the bottle! Most of the time, the labels are not readable due to the temperature or bottles being rubbed together in transit.

Even if they say they will attend, by the time they think about coming, they have forgotten which church handed them the water in the first place.

Mistake 4: Home Bible Studies

This next subject is going to be hard for some of you, and my intention is not to be abrasive or provide discouragement. For many years, the only method of soul winning we have ever been told to be effective is home Bible studies. And I realize it has been effective to some degree. However, our goal is to find the most *effective* ways to win the world.

I have taught hundreds, if not thousands, of Bible studies. I have won some people through this method. It wasn't until recently, I realized something.

Things to Avoid

I looked back at all the times that I spent teaching these Bible studies to win souls, and I realized there are not many souls who ever truly even finished the study.

I would spend weeks teaching one or two people a 12-week Bible study and as soon as we approached the lesson on salvation and baptism, there seemed to be roadblock. The people who I had spent so much time in their homes, loving and listening to, would usually start making excuses as to why they couldn't make the next study.

I learned many years later why this was. You see, most of the content of the home Bible studies we have today are doctrinal based. They are designed for the most part to teach the doctrine of the Pentecostal faith.

We have to realize that when we are teaching these people, they are not even born again. They are not even babies in the eyes of God. So when we teach them doctrine, it's basically giving them spiritual meat. When you give babies meat, they, no doubt, will choke on it and die.

That was what was happening in most of the cases of Bible studies I had taught. We must give them milk. We must use the basic plan of salvation and get them to the John 3:5 experience of being born again before teaching them everything we can about being Pentecostal.

I have a theory. If we could ever get these people to fall in love with Jesus, truly learning to love and worship him, he will teach them to love Pentecost! So here is our dilemma: let's say we have one man, and we spend 12 weeks teaching him a Bible study. Then, on lesson 9 he gets upset and never has another study. We have 9 weeks of time invested in this person with no results.

We suggest a more effective way, the "Heaven or Hell" method. This allows someone to respond to salvation immediately, being born again of the water and spirit. Usually you can win several people per day.

So, let's say for one week you went out trying to win souls using the "Heaven or Hell" method. You would most likely have five to ten people repent, be baptized, and filled with the Holy Ghost that week.

Now take those five to ten people and get them into a basic Bible study as a form of discipleship instead of a method of soul winning!

When you get to the lesson on salvation, there will be no fear. No one will quit the Bible study. They will rejoice because they have already done what is required!

I want to say one more time; I am not saying these methods will not work. There are churches that have grown almost entirely by teaching home Bible studies. We are suggesting there are more effective ways, based on time and energy, to bring the largest harvest into the kingdom of God.

Chapter 12

Bus and Van Ministry

Why are we missing it when it comes to bus ministry? Jesus said, "Suffer the children unto me." Yes, it's hard work, but look at the lives that we could help change!

This is one place where I believe the devil has deceived the church the greatest. When he tricked us into believing bus and Van Ministry was no longer effective and worth the cost, he won a huge battle against the church!

Ladies and gentlemen, let me be real clear. This is probably the most effective and important ministry in the church! We must get back to making bus and van ministry the priority of the church!

Over our lifetime of winning souls, I can testify that literally thousands and thousands of people have told me they do not go to church because they have no way to get there!

Wow. So multitudes of souls will face eternity in a lake of fire because the churches of the living God thought it was more important to spend money on every other object in the church than transporting souls to the house of God?

Bus and Van Ministry

I am from northwest Indiana, also the home of the First
Baptist Church of Hammond, Indiana. This church was
commonly known for years as the largest Sunday School in
the world! In 1975, they held a bus ministry contest bringing
in over 30,560 people!

The church ran over 230 buses using 1,000 people to work the
routes each week. You couldn't go anywhere within a 75-mile
radius of that church on a Saturday or Sunday without either
being invited or seeing one of their busses!

Today the largest church in the World is in Brooklyn, New
York and is lead by Pastor Bill Wilson of Metro Ministries.
Pastor Wilson personally drives a church bus every Sunday to
pick up children and they minister to over 20,000 children
every Sunday!

Why are we missing it when it comes to bus ministry? Jesus
said, "Suffer the children unto me!" Yes, it's hard work, but
look at the lives that we could help change!

Every member of our churches should at least be filling their
cars and automobiles up with children every week. Children
love to come to Sunday School. Maybe they are bad, maybe
they are not clean, but how will they ever get better if
someone doesn't love them and show them the love of Jesus!

We should have our parking lots filled with busses and vans.
There is not a church in America that could not double in one
year if they would put a priority on bus and van ministry in
their city.

Bus and Van Ministry

Getting Started

To operate a bus or van ministry effectively, you should have teams that are given certain geographical areas of your city to reach. Make sure the teams work their area each week and never miss visitation. There should be a minimum of five people per team. This way if a couple have vacation or have to miss; someone will be there to keep the route going.

If you miss one week of visitation or picking up the people, you will fail at your ministry. Most of the people you reach are so used to neglect and unfaithful promises; you will just become part of the same club in their mind if you miss a week.

Your teams should start out working the largest apartment complex in your city. You want to work apartment complexes because they are where you will bring the most people from per square mile.

If possible, it's a good idea to have a block party in the neighborhood the week before starting the bus route. People can become acquainted with you and the church. Be sure to give away a few prizes and try and provide free hamburgers or pizza with a drink at the block party.

Most pizza places have $5 pizzas now, and if you ask them to cut them into slices of 10 per pizza, you can feed 500 people for $250.

Bus and Van Ministry

For instance, if you have a 500-unit apartment complex in your city, the average amount of people per unit is listed at four so potentially in one stop of your bus route you are looking to reach over 2,000 people. We know from experience the average amount of souls in one unit is way more than four.

Your job would be to go there every Saturday with bags of fruit snacks or candy and flyers announcing the service. Spend at least one hour per complex visiting and encouraging people to come.

Be sure and keep a list of those who have attended and visit with them first each week. Make sure if there is no one home that you at least leave a flyer to let him or her know you stopped by. Make sure the time is on the flyer of your route pick-up so they can be ready.

You will want to try and get to these apartments at least one and a half hour early on Sunday. You will find that sometimes it's hard to get people to the place where they are ready and waiting. Remember they are babies. It will take a while for them to become mature in God.

Also remember, these children are not going to be angels. They need God; so don't expect them to be the best behaved. It will take time and patience.

Make sure you keep an attendance log each week and try and reward children for faithful attendance. Also offer them extra candy if they will bring a friend. You will find that bus routes are not just for children, many of the adults will want to come as well. Encourage children to bring their parents and make use of our "Sunday School Seed" program listed in our *10 Effective Ways to Win Souls* chapter.

Bus and Van Ministry

Make sure your church has amazing Sunday School. Try to make it as fun and educational as much as possible. It may be a good idea to have plenty of snacks on hand each week to feed the children before service. You can have songs and games while the children enjoy a snack. You will find that your snack might be the only meal they have for the whole day.

If you do not have money to buy a bus or van, sell your church sound system, sell your car, sell your instruments, take out a loan, re-finance the church or whatever it takes. We owe it to these children to share the love of Christ to them and do our best to reach them! The more your bus routes grow, the more of your city you can cover. Start out small, fill up the busses and vans you have, and then expand to a larger area.

Try and influence people from your church to get their CDL drivers endorsement. Also, every new convert should be taught that they are a part of ministry and they should work on their CDL endorsement as well. Make it a common interest of the church.

Bus and van ministry is probably the hardest work in reaching the lost, but it is the most rewarding as well. You will never have as much joy in serving God, as you will when one of these children you reached for become a pastor or minister in your church!

Every child in your city deserves our very best attempt at presenting the gospel to save them from the lake of fire! Will you go?

Chapter 13

10 Effective Ways to Win Souls

Winning Souls #1: Backslider or Prodigal Program

We must strive to reach every soul we can. We must not just strive for the upper and middle class white American; we must reach for every human being alive today.

This is a program designed to reach out to all of the backsliders in your area.

You will want to design a list with columns for *name, address,* and *phone number.* Have this list in a place where people can easily access it to add their information.

Each service, make an announcement. Ask anyone to add to the sheet information of any backslider who should be contacted by the church.

Once the list is complete, one person from the church who can work well with database information should enter all of the names and information into a worksheet on Excel.

Once the information is entered, the next step will be to prepare packets to be sent out in the mail to each person on the list.

Someone from the media department should make up a CD with old songs and hymns. Older song styles are effective because most of the backsliders have been gone so long they will not relate to today's style of music.

You will also want to purchase some basic cards from Hallmark or any card company and write a simple few words like, "We're thinking about you and can't wait to see you again."

Writing something like that will let them know the church loves them and they are welcome back!

The person working with the database will keep track of the information sent out.

On your first mailing, you will send a music CD with the Hallmark card.

Then every month thereafter, you will only send another card.

The person working with the database will also print out a sheet with every prodigal's name on it and pass those sheets out to the church members to use as prayer guides to call the names of these prodigals out each day in prayer.

It will be nearly impossible for the backsliders to stay gone when you pray for them each day!

Winning Souls #2: Sunday School Seed Program

This program reaches into the homes of our Sunday School children through a packet that is created to send home as a seed.

93

Basically you will make up folders and send them home with the oldest child in a family and ask them to give it to their parents. This program is very effective and is a great way to reach the parents of the children! You can get the folders at any office store. They have the pockets on the inside. Here is what we suggest putting in these folders:

    a. Music CD with old style songs

    b. Bible Study (Tim's Bible Study is free and effective)

    c. Letter from pastor

    d. Church bulletin if you have one each week

    e. Church schedule of services or events calendar

    f. McDonald's gift cards, if affordable

    g. Prayer cloth

Winning Souls #3: Court House Program

This program is very effective. You want to have a couple of elderly people working in this program.

You will need to find out the schedule at the courthouse for all of the court sessions including criminal, divorce, bankruptcy, and traffic.

Then, order a sign. Usually you can get one from a restaurant equipment store online. Get one that has those small letters that you can stick in the grooves and write things. Your sign should say, "Prayer Requests Taken Here."

You will also want to go to an office supply store and order a nice nametag. On the tag, you will have your name and "Prayer Requests Taken Here".

Finally, you will need a guest book. This can be any kind of guest book you can find, as you will use this book to record the prayer request information, the person's name, address, and phone number for further follow-up or a nice letter from the pastor.

You will want to meet with the court bailiff to let him know your intentions. Be sure to let him know you will not be disruptive and you will respect the wishes of the court.

Once you have permission, be sure and make as many sessions as possible. People will get to know you and trust you.

Remember people in these situations are hurting. They need someone with faith and someone who will show kindness and mercy.

You will not only reach the person going to court, but often they will have a lot of family members there with them for support.

Make a good impression, be as kind as possible, hug people, and love them. You will also want to have a large supply of church cards with the service times and phone number of the church. Hand these out to as many people as possible!

Bring your guest book back, pray for the names you have recorded, and ask God to help each person.

Winning Souls #4: Free Cooking Class

Your ladies auxiliary or group in your church can start this program. It can be an outreach tool as well as a discipleship tool.

Each week, a different lady from your group can bring a small recipe on an index card along with the ingredients to make her recipe.

The person teaching the recipe would hand out blank index cards to the people in attendance, asking them to write down each ingredient.

While the person is instructing the group on what to write down, they will also be actually making their recipe as they go along.

For instance, if I were to teach the class, and my recipe was brownies, I would hand out blank cards and then tell the group to write down the following ingredients:

1 cup vegetable oil
2 cups sugar
2 teaspoons vanilla
4 large eggs
1/2 teaspoon baking powder
2/3 cup coco powder
1/2 teaspoon salt
1 cup flour

Then I would give the instructions on preparation:
- Preheat your oven to 350 degrees while you are preparing the brownie mix.
- Mix the oil, sugar, eggs, and vanilla until they are well blended.
- Mix all the dry ingredients together separately.
- Add the dry ingredients to the egg mixture.
- Pour into a 9x13-baking dish or pan.
- Bake for about 30 minutes or until the brownies start to separate from the edges of the baking dish or pan.
- Let cool and enjoy.

While I was telling the class how to make them, I would actually be preparing the dish and placing it in the oven.

Now, if you do not have a kitchen facility, you can also use recipes that do not need to be cooked, or use a microwave or an outdoor grill.

While the dish is cooking, take time to fellowship. Put on soft music and make lots of friends!

Once the dish is complete, take it out, let it cool, and then serve it to all of your guests!

Before they eat, always ask them to bow their heads to pray. Do not just pray a simple prayer. Call down the fire from heaven and ask God to touch each guest! You will be shocked at how many of them began to weep, cry, and repent! You will pray many through to the Holy Ghost right there in the kitchen! Then take them and baptize them right away!

You will want to prepare a small flyer on the brightest yellow paper you can find, highlighting in large letter, "Free Cooking Class." Make it simple and do not use any church lingo.

Hand these flyers out to all your new converts. Also pass them out at all the women's shelters, battered women's facilities, WIC offices, and welfare offices. Try and have your classes on a weeknight at 7 pm.

Winning Souls #5: Learn the English Language for FREE!

We must strive to reach every soul we can. We must not just strive for the upper and middle class white American; we must reach for every human being alive today!

God has no place for racism and prejudice in the Kingdom of God. He is no respecter of person, and neither should we be.

To reach every nationality in our day, we must extend a helping hand. We must offer to assist these wonderful people and help them become a part of our society. One of the greatest needs in helping people who have come to our nation is to help them learn the English language.

You can go online to the free language translator sites and translate almost any language to the English language.

We suggest choosing a nationality that is prominent in your area. For instance, if you have a lot of Hispanic people, you will make up a flyer using Spanish and advertise, "Learn the English Language for Free. Includes Free Meal." You will use bright yellow paper with black letters and keep it simple. Make sure the address is clear and in large print.

You will take these flyers to all of the local places that the Hispanic people congregate and do business with. For example, Mexican restaurants, laundry mats, Spanish grocery stores are all Hispanic locales. Leave the flyers out for people to take one and try and get the storeowners to help you promote the event.

We recommend having the class at 7 pm on a weeknight.

The good thing is you do not have to know Spanish or any other language to teach this class. Of course, if you have someone who can speak Spanish, it's a blessing. You will actually learn Spanish along with the class while they are learning English!

You will want to go online each week before your class starts and choose 10 easy words. Try and find common words that are used often in sentences. Once you have the words, go to one of the translation sites and translate your word from English to Spanish. Print that information on a sheet of paper so you will have 10 words and there translation.

Go to the class and be as friendly as possible, even if you cannot speak their language. Love has its own language, and people can tell if it's real!

Love the people, share the handout with them, and carefully read the words in English then Spanish. After class, take the people who show up to the fellowship area and feed them tacos, rice, and whatever cultural food that fits.

Winning Souls #6: Sunday School Give-away Crusade

This program is very effective in cultivating multitudes of first time guests. The more guests you have showing up in your service, the livelier and exciting your services will be! Not only will they be lively, but also you will have people to reach for and see lives transformed each week. Every week

10 Effective Ways to Win Souls

we should strive to bring in as many first time guests as possible.

Some people will say that people are just coming for the give-aways. I say, who cares why they are coming, at least they

are hearing the Gospel and have an opportunity to be in the presence of a merciful God!

You will want to set up your print materials with the same information on the flyers and door hangers. We recommend something like "Blessing the Community through Giving. We have a sample of the flyer and door hanger on our website, www.gowinsouls.com. Go to *download* then *soul-winning materials.*

It is extremely important not to put a bunch of religious wording on your advertisements. Avoid words such as *revival, Holy Ghost Crusade, evangelist, miracles,* or *Acts 2:28.* You get the picture.

To set up this crusade, you will want to have a 2 pm service. You will want to make up 1,000 to 2,000 flyers using the brightest yellow paper you can buy. Set it up where you will print two flyers per page, on an 8½ x 11 sheets. Print the images in the landscape layout, cutting the sheet in half, allowing for two flyers per sheet of paper. You may also want to print these double sided with English on one side and Spanish on the other.

You will also want to order 3,000 to 5,000 door hangers. Again, there is a company out of Destin, Florida, we use called www.topvalueprinting.com that gives the best deal on printing. They will print 5,000 bright yellow door hangers and ship them for only $212. They also will print the flyers.

Once you have the flyers, organize a large group of people to work on a Saturday hanging the door hangers and passing out the flyers.

You will want to hit apartment complexes first. They will have the most effect because of the amount of people you can reach from such a small geographical area.

You can go to www.mapquest.com and enter *Apartments* in the search box. It will bring up almost all of the complexes in your city.

You will want to give away prizes at the end of the service. We always give away the following:

Ten - $10 Gas Cards
Four- $25 Wal-Mart cards
One – Bicycle – BMX style
Two – Key Chain Digital Cameras
One – MP3 Player
30 – Dollar Store toys
(Usually the $2 toys: 15 boys and 15 girls things such as jump ropes, bubbles, coloring books, etc...)

It is important to wait until the complete end of service to give away gifts. Don't worry, people will stay. If you have 25 families in your church who will commit to giving a donation of $100 through a period of one year, you can have a bike give away each week and be known as the church that gives away bicycles! In the service, you will want to play old songs, like *Amazing Grace, I'll Fly Away, Jesus on the Main Line.* Keep them old, because most of the people you will have in service have no Pentecostal background. They will not relate to the new music our churches play today. They will sit like statues!

Preach about ten minutes on sin, its wages and what it does to people's lives, and then preach ten minutes on salvation, keeping it simple. Center the message on John 3:5 and Acts 2:38. Ask everyone who is there to come to the front of the building. Once they are there, tell them what they need to do to repent and be baptized.

You will want to choose several apartment complexes that you can basically adopt. You will want to visit there each week, taking fruit snacks or some type of free candy each week and a flyer. Stay in contact with the children! You can purchase boxes of fruit snacks from Sam's Club for $9 per box. Each box has 72 packages of fruit snacks in them, and they are very effective to give to people when they open the door to a conversation. The brand name is *Members Mark Fruit Snacks.*

Winning Souls #7: Witnessing in Restaurants

Now this may come to a surprise to many, but as Pentecostals we love to eat! Amen? At least that's how I have observed things in my walk with God!

I would like to share some information that may make your time eating-out more profitable. As we are out in places eating, this is a great time to really become witnesses! What most people do not realize is that we have one of the best opportunities to share our faith with people when we are out in restaurants!

You see, the person who serves you has to pretty much be at your service the whole time you are there. This allows a great chance to share the love of God! Your server will more than likely be glad to listen to what you have to say, they are somewhat of a captive audience. Pray before you enter a restaurant that God will help you become a better witness, and you will see results.

There are a few things that need to be said of this type of ministry. First of all, as I have stated, your server will be there to listen to you and to serve your needs. This can be a bad thing as well as a good one.

You see, I have noticed over the years some bad things that are being done in restaurants. People complain, they act foolish, allow their children to act foolish, and make a huge mess. It is very important that you do not give your church a bad reputation by demanding things or being snobbish and rude to these people.

My mother worked as a server in a restaurant for more than 20 years. She, on more than one occasion, told me stories of a certain church group that came in once a week. She really dreaded waiting on these people because they would be so rude and would demand things in a really mean way. They also would leave little or no tip. Tipping is another topic needing to be addressed. If you are out in a place like this, you need to be generous with your gratuity. You have to really place yourself in the shoes of these people, how would you look at us if we acted in such a way and then left a small tip? Would you want to come to our church? Would you desire to know what we have inside us? The resounding answer would be no.

Be respectful. Say, "May I please, thank you very much, excuse me." You know, proper manners! We are shining lights, and when we are out in a restaurant we need to let our lights shine!

Jesus is coming back soon. We need to be more concerned about the people around us and where they may be headed. We have a responsibility to reach the lost, to love our neighbor.

How can we say we love these people if we know that they are lost and we do nothing to reach them? It's time to go to work ladies and gentlemen! Let's all do our part to win someone. Let us have compassion and a renewed burden for the lost! We have but a short time!

Here are a few tips and ideas you may ponder.

a. Sometime during your meal, hand your server a tract, a Bible study, or a contact card with your church information and service times.

b. Leave a *sizable* tip to show you care for the server's hard work. Even if the service was not up to your expectations, do not complain. Do not leave a small tip. They will not recognize their failure, but they will recognize your lack of concern for them.

c. Be as polite and loving as you possibly can. This is a soul, and there is nothing more important than that. Do not be selfish; have the mind of Christ!

d. Make sure your children are well behaved! Do not allow them to run all over the place and make a mess. Do not allow them to be rude to the server. Try and clean up any extra messes that your children make, and apologize to your server for the inconvenience.

e. Smile! Allow this person see that there is joy in serving God! Who wants to go to a church where there are rude, cheap, inconsiderate people? I know I wouldn't want to.

f. Do not be shy to share your testimony. You have been brought a long way. This person needs to have a chance to become born again!

Winning Souls #8: Youth Outreach Program

If you have ten young people that can donate $5 for soul winning, take the $50 to any pizza franchise and get five large pizzas for $25. This is plenty of pizza for 25 to 30 people. Then you buy two to three 12-packs of Coke and Mountain Dew, costing another $15, leaving $10 left to go to Wal-Mart and buy a cheap basketball or any sport item.

Now you have pizza, soft drinks, and a basketball. Take it to a park where there are a lot of people playing ball and announce you are having a free pizza party with a basketball give-away. You will meet tons of new friends, eat pizza with them, and witness! Be sure you take church guest registration cards, church cards, and flyers with you. You will use the guest cards to get information, telling the people it's for the basketball give away.

Once everyone signs up and you eat, have one of the guests draw the guest card for the winner. Now, you have all the information from the people who were glad to give it to you so they could win a ball. Your youth have had fun and ate pizza and witnessed and it only cost them $5!

Winning Souls #9: Sticky Notes

You can purchase sticky notes in bright yellow and have your church info printed on it for less than 1 cent per sticky note.

You will want to make sure that the top line of text is in large letters and says "Invitation". You will want to list the church service times, phone number, web address if you have one, and any other info. It is not recommended that you put a bunch of church words like *revival, Acts 2:38, one God, Jesus' name.* Yes, we believe that to be the message; however, someone out of the world who reads your sticky note for the first time will not know what any of that means.

You can use these sticky notes all over! Pass out stacks of 100 to each family and have them start sticking them everywhere! Here is one web site that carries these: http://www.bizforms.com/postit.htm

Winning Souls #10: Hospital Ministry

You will need to purchase 50 to 100 small gift bags. You can find them on most any search engine by typing in *wholesale gift bags.*

Once you have them, you will need to purchase travel size Scope mouthwash, Chap stick, lotions, fingernail clippers, and candy.

You will also want to order some pre-cut prayer clothes, or have someone from your church cut them. You can also buy them from the Internet with your church name, address, and phone number on them, which I suggest.

Place all of these items in the bags, along with a church card and a card with your service times, and take them to the local hospital. You just go to every room where someone is staying and hand them the gift bag and tell them you will be praying for them.

Chapter 14

Closing Thoughts

As I try to bring this book to a close, my heart is heavy. I can only think of the souls that could be reached if the church is awakened, and a new passion and burden is lit like fire shut up in our bones!

There are over 6.5 billion souls alive today on earth! We have a tremendous job ahead of us. We can make a difference. Over 2,000 years ago, The Apostles turned all of Asia upside down with the Gospel with just a few Christians. What could we do with millions of Apostolic, Holy Ghost-filled believers if we set our priorities to reach this world?

We will never reach the multitudes from inside of our buildings. We will never reach them by only living a separate and holy lifestyle. If we are to reach them, it will be the biblical way of going into the highways and byways and compelling and persuading them to come in!

I want you to think of something for just a minute. I want you to close your eyes for 15 seconds and get a clear picture of the most loved person that is alive today in your life. Once you have that picture, open your eyes and read this next paragraph.

Closing Thoughts

As you are driving home, you arrive at your street to see your house on fire. As you look up, you can see the loved one that you just had a picture of in your mind. That loved one is standing in the window screaming for help, there are flames all around, and there is very little time to act.

When you pull up to the house, what would you personally do to bring your loved one to safety?

Would you risk your life? Would you care who was watching? Would you do anything you could to bring them to safety?

Of course you would! You wouldn't stop until they were rescued!

Now, let's change the story. Let's say your loved one is in the house, and they only have a few moments to live. They are screaming and crying for help, fire is all around, smoke is choking them, and they are facing certain death if not rescued.

A fire truck pulls up outside of your home. On the truck are the tools to bring your loved one to safety without any real effort. There is a hose to put out the flame, a ladder to climb up and bring your loved one down, an ax to break down the door; everything is in the truck for a successful rescue.

Something strange is happening. The fireman stays in the truck. He is asking himself, *should I risk harm to go save that person? I wonder if it's too dangerous.* He then thinks, *well maybe I should go back to the firehouse and get more training on saving people before I try this.*

Or maybe he sees a "no soliciting" sign or a "no trespassing" sign and wonders if he should avoid going up to the home for fear of getting yelled at.

Maybe he looks at the person in danger and thinks he would be bothering them, they would make fun of his uniform, or they might not really want to be saved.

So instead of getting out of the truck to easily bring your loved one to safety, he drives away and heads to the closest restaurant to fellowship with the other firemen. He leaves your loved one to die in the flames.

What would you want to do to the fireman if he let your loved one die?

What do you think the world should want to do to us when each week, we head to the spiritual firehouse to get more training while passing by hundreds of people facing eternity and hell?

What do you think the world thinks of us as we pass them, ignoring every soul around us to get to the restaurant for fellowship?

I realize this is a very hard thing to think about, but how true is this? What about the lost world? When is the last time you personally won a soul?

Have we allowed the cares of life to harden our hearts towards the lost souls of this world?

Everyone I talk to says they love souls and they want to win souls; however, many of them never even try. Have we been deceived?

Closing Thoughts

Look around your church. How many new souls are there that you personally brought in? Then look around your city. Find out the population of your city and think about how many souls will face hell if someone doesn't get a burden and go reach them.

You can win souls! You can change your city! You need to do whatever you have to do to realize this and wake up before it's too late! It will be worth the cost! Go on a fast, pray until you weep over the souls of your city, and lay aside everything that gets in the way of outreach and soul winning.

It's not God's will that any should perish; he has paid a price for their soul. Would you reach them?

I pray this book will allow your soul to be stirred. Please do not resist the Holy Ghost. God is trying to use you to reach others!

I cannot imagine how any person with the Holy Ghost can possibly be comfortable in letting souls go to hell day after day without taking out your spiritual tools to help rescue them!

GO! Go with passion and love. Rescue every soul, pulling them from the lake of fire!

Soul Winning Quotes

"I care not where I go or how I live or what I endure so that I may save souls. When I sleep I dream of them; when I awake they are first in my thoughts...no amount of scholastic attainment, or able and profound exposition, of brilliant and stirring eloquence can atone for the absence of a deep, impassioned, sympathetic love for human souls."
- David Brainerd

"Some men's ambition is art, some men's ambition is fame, some men's ambition is gold.
My ambition is the souls of men."
– William Booth

"Send me to the nearest place to the bottomless pit."
– Gipsy Smith

"'Not called,' did you say? 'Not heard the call,' I think you should say. Put your ear down to the Bible and hear Him bid you go and pull sinners out of the fire of sin. Put your ear down to the burdened, agonized heart of humanity and listen to its pitiful wail for help. Go stand by the gates of Hell and hear the damned entreat you to go to their fathers' houses and bid their brothers and sister and servants and master not to come there. Then look Christ in the face – whose mercy you have professed to obey – and tell Him whether you will join heart and soul and body and circumstances in the march to publish His mercy to the world."
– William Booth

Soul Winning Quotes

"If you found a cure for cancer, wouldn't it be inconceivable to hide it from the rest of mankind? How much more inconceivable to keep silent about the cure from the eternal wages of sin, which is death."
- Dave Davidson

"If we do not catch men, we are in great danger of losing even the desire to catch them. Our purposed activity is in peril of becoming a dream."
- J.H. Jowett

"To every lost soul, Christ says: "Come unto me." To every redeemed soul, Christ says: Go for me."
- Unknown

"The Great Commission is not an option to be considered; it is a command to be obeyed."
– Hudson Taylor

"We are praying for sinners to come to God; God is pleading with saints to go for sinners."
– Unknown

"There is no greater honor than to be the instrument in God's hands of leading one person out of the kingdom of Satan into the glorious light of heaven."
- Dwight L. Moody

Soul Winning Quotes

"I have disposed of all my property to my family. There is one thing more I wish I could give to them, and that is the Christian religion. If they had that, and I had not given them one cent, they would be rich. If they have not that, and I had given them the world, they would be poor."
– Patrick Henry

"...the chief duty of every father is to bring his children to God."
– Rufus C. Burleson

"This generation of Christians is responsible for this generation of souls on the earth!"
– Keith Green

"Some want to live within the sound of church or chapel bell; I want to run a rescue shop within a yard of hell."
- C.T. Studd

"Answering a student's question, 'Will the heathen who have not heard the Gospel be saved?' thus, It is more a question with me whether we, who have the Gospel and fail to give it to those who have not, can be saved."
– Charles Spurgeon

"Evangelism is not a professional job for a few trained men, but is instead the unrelenting responsibility of every person who belongs to the company of Jesus."
- Elton Trueblood

Soul Winning Quotes

You have nothing to do but to save souls. Therefore spend
and be spent in this work. And go not only to those that need
you, but to those that need you most. It is not your business
to preach so many times, and to take care of this or that
society; but to save as many souls as you can; to bring as
many sinners as you possibly can to repentance.
– John Wesley

Could a mariner sit idle if he heard the drowning cry? Could
a doctor sit in comfort and just let his patients die? Could a
fireman sit idle, let men burn and give no hand? Can you sit
at ease in Zion with the world around you damned?
– Leonard Ravenhill

30 Scripture Passages on Soul Winning

Matthew 4:19

And he saith unto them, Follow me, and I will make
<u>you</u> fishers of men.
*If we're not fishing for men who are we following? This
statement is to individuals, notice the "you."*

Luke 19:10

For the Son of man is come to seek and to save
that which was lost.
*To be a Christian means to be like Christ, how can we say we
are like Christ if we do not seek to save the lost?*

Ezekiel 3:18

When I say unto the wicked, Thou shalt surely die; and thou
givest him not warning, nor speakest to warn the wicked
from his wicked way, to save his life; the same wicked
man shall die in his iniquity; but his blood
will I require at thine hand.

Ezekiel 3:20

Again, When a righteous man doth turn from his
righteousness, and commit iniquity, and I lay a stumbling-
block before him, he shall die: because thou hast not given
him warning, he shall die in his sin, and his righteousness
which he hath done shall not be remembered;
but his blood will I require at thine hand.

30 Scripture Passages on Soul Winning

Ezekiel 33:6
But if the watchman see the sword come, and blow not the trumpet, and the people be not warned; if the sword come, and take any person from among them, he is taken away in his iniquity; but his blood will I require
at the watchman's hand.

Ezekiel 33:8
When I say unto the wicked, O wicked man, thou shalt surely die; if thou dost not speak to warn the wicked from his way, that wicked man shall die in his iniquity; but his blood will I require at thine hand.

Proverbs 11:30
The fruit of the righteous is a tree of life; and he
that winneth souls is wise.
What's that make the man that does not win souls? Foolish.

Matthew 25:26
His lord answered and said unto him, Thou wicked and slothful servant, thou knewest that I reap where I sowed not, and gather where I have not strawed:

Proverbs 10:5
He that gathereth in summer is a wise son: but he that sleepeth in harvest is a son that causeth shame.

30 Scripture Passages on Soul Winning

John 14:15
If ye love me, keep my commandments.
The Lord commands us to GO and make disciples and reach
our world. Also it says that the second greatest
commandment of all is to love your neighbor as yourself.
If we love ourselves enough to be in church and
be saved where is our neighbor?

James 4:17
Therefore to him that knoweth to do good, and doeth it not, to
him it is sin.

II Cor. 5:11
Knowing, therefore, the terror of the Lord,
we persuade men.

Luke 14:23
And the lord said unto the servant, Go out into the highways
and hedges, and compel them to come in, that my
house may be filled.

Matthew 10:7
And as ye go, preach, saying, The kingdom of
heaven is at hand.

Mark 16:15
And he said unto them, Go ye into all the world, and preach
the gospel to every creature.

30 Scripture Passages on Soul Winning

Acts 1:8
But ye shall receive power, after that the Holy Ghost is come upon you: and ye shall be witnesses unto me both in Jerusalem, and in all Judaea, and in Samaria, and unto the uttermost part of the earth.
The Holy Ghost will be the power to make us become witnesses.

2 Timothy 3:5
Having a form of godliness, but denying the power thereof: from such turn away.
This tells us that there will be a group of people on the earth who have a form of godliness. They don't smoke, cuss, they wear Godly apparel, live holy, but they deny the power to become witnesses!

Daniel 12:3
And they that be wise shall shine as the brightness of the firmament; and they that turn many to righteousness as the stars forever and ever.

John 4:35-36
35 Say not ye, There are yet four months, and then cometh harvest? behold, I say unto you, Lift up your eyes, and look on the fields; for they are white already to harvest.
36 And he that reapeth receiveth wages, and gathereth fruit unto life eternal: that both he that soweth and he that reapeth may rejoice together.

30 Scripture Passages on Soul Winning

Matthew 28:19
Go ye therefore, and teach all nations, baptizing them in the name of the Father, and of the Son, and of the Holy Ghost:

Luke 15:10
Likewise, I say unto you, there is joy in the presence of the angels of God over one sinner that repenteth.
It's not the angels that get joy, it's God himself! Now watch what happens when a soul winner brings someone in and they repent. It gives God great joy.

Nehemiah 8:10
...for the joy of the LORD is your strength.

Acts 22:15
For thou shalt be his witness unto all men of what thou hast seen and heard.

John 15:5
I am the vine, ye are the branches: He that abideth in me, and I in him, the same bringeth forth much fruit: for without me ye can do nothing.

Psalm 1:3
And he shall be like a tree planted by the rivers of water, that bringeth forth his fruit in his season; his leaf also shall not wither; and whatsoever he doeth shall prosper.

30 Scripture Passages on Soul Winning

Acts 5:42

And daily in the temple, and in every house, they ceased not
to teach and preach Jesus Christ.

*We call ourselves Apostolic; this is what the apostolic people
did in the Bible!*

Matthew 9:36

But when he saw the multitudes, he was moved with
compassion on them, because they fainted, and were
scattered abroad, as sheep having no shepherd.

This is how Jesus sees the lost!

Psalm 126:6

He that goeth forth and weepeth, bearing precious seed, shall
doubtless come again with rejoicing, bringing his sheaves
with him.

Excuses

In our travels and experiences working and winning souls, we have probably heard most every excuse possible for why people don't win others. I wanted to provide a few here so you will be ready for what's going to come your way. I think it's important to be ready for this to prevent disappointments.

You see, even in the Bible you can read of people making excuses.

Luke 14:18-20
And they all with one *consent* began to make excuse. The first said unto him, I have bought a piece of ground, and I must needs go and see it: I pray thee have me excused. And another said, I have bought five yoke of oxen, and I go to prove them: I pray thee have me excused. And another said, I have married a wife, and therefore I cannot come.

Just like today, people seem to have every excuse for not participating in the harvest. We can make a difference we just have to GO!

Common Excuses Used

"We're too busy to go out on outreach."
– *But not too busy to go hunting, fishing, shopping, browsing the Internet, or any other leisurely hobbies.*

"That kind of outreach won't work in our city."
– *How do you know if you're not willing to try it?*

"We're not outgoing type of people."
– *You don't have a hard time pushing the person in front of you out of the sale line, or yelling at the umpire in your child's soccer game.*

Excuses

"My family time is important; I need to spend my time with them."
– *You need to get your family into the field of harvest. "Train up a child the way they should go."*

"We don't want to offend people so we will just advertise on a billboard."
– *Guess you're comfortable letting people go to hell?*

"We cannot afford to do outreach."
– *You cannot afford not to! It's strange how we have all kinds of money for sound equipment, instruments, costumes for drama, etc...but no money for outreach.*

"We will just be lifestyle evangelists. People will see us looking and acting different and want to come."
– *Really? How's that working out so far? Is your church filled with sinners every week wanting to be like you?*

I'm sure this part will probably anger some people, mostly the ones who have been using these excuses. I'm not writing these to make you angry, I'm writing this to help us get real about outreach and winning souls.

If we feel like our excuses are worthwhile, we could be in great danger of making the Master angry.

Luke 14:21
So that servant came, and shewed his lord these things. Then the master of the house *being angry* said to his servant, Go out quickly into the streets and lanes of the city, and bring in hither the poor, and the maimed, and the halt, and the blind.

Excuses

Let's go into all of the world and preach the gospel to every creature! You are a SOUL WINNER!

Galatians 4:16
Have I now become your enemy by telling you the truth?

Heaven or Hell Method

(The soul winner approaches someone and hands them a card or flyer.)
Soul winner: Do you have one of these flyers? Are you busy now?
Individual: No, I don't have one.
Soul Winner: Do you want to go to heaven or hell?
Individual: Heaven
Soul winner: That's awesome! That's where everyone should want to go! Everyone says heaven but most people never do what it takes to get there. Are you sure you want to go to heaven?
Individual: Yes, I'm sure. I want to go to heaven.
Soul winner: John 3:5 says, "Except a man be born again of the water and the spirit you cannot enter the kingdom of heaven." Say CAN NOT for me."
Individual: Can not
Soul winner: It takes about five minutes to repent, and 10 minutes to be baptized the right way so God can fill you with the Holy Ghost. What would stop you from coming to do those two things right now?
(Most of the time the individual will answer by saying, either nothing, or that they have already been baptized. When a person tells you they have already been baptized, the normal thing for apostolic people to do is ask them if it was in Jesus name and when they say "no", we start beating them over the head with our Bible and scriptures telling them how they will go to hell being baptized that way! Avoid this. Here is the way to handle it....)
Soul winner: Oh, you were baptized already? Do you remember if they said in the name of the father, son and Holy Ghost?
(Most people have no idea what they said and whatever you ask them, they will agree to it. That's why we never ask them if they were baptized in Jesus name, because most people will just say "yes." Then what do you do with them? If they say yes to father, son and Holy Ghost, give them a big high five.)
Soul winner: Awesome! I have some good news and some bad news. The bad news is that you weren't baptized the right way. The good news is that you can get baptized right now the right way so you can go to heaven. What would stop you tonight from being baptized the right way?
(Most of the time they will say nothing, so you tell them you have a church, you have clothes to change into, and you can baptize now.)

We want to give a special thank you, as we honor the following people who have sponsored the printing of this book!

Keith Ladner	Robert & Erica Fletcher
Brenda Beach	Brandon & Calandra King
Edward Hutchison	Wes & Karissa Cordell
Jason Vause	Erik & Elsa Webster
John Billingsley	Tyler Crow
Matt Maddix	Charles and Tammy Rhodus
Randall Barnes	Duke Sherman
Dr. Jeff & Renee Stirnemann	The God Squad
Jason & Jamie Rasor	Brandon & Amy McGuire
Edward Hosmer	Brigitte Swift
John Bernadini II	Jeff & Heidi Cecil
Life Way Church	www.apostolicbiblestudies.us
Danny & Rebecca Anderson	Ron & Rennie, Caleb Beasley
Grace Apostolic Church – Clawson MI.	David Toler